CONTENTS

The journey of Quantum Spirituality	1
A Personal Note from the Author	4
Chapter 1: The Eternal Dance of the Quantum and the Divine	7
Chapter 2: The Celestial Tapestry of Existence	14
Chapter 3: The Holographic Nature of the Universe	23
Chapter 4: The Quantum Mind: Consciousness as the Bedrock of Existence	32
Chapter 5: The Quantum Leap: From Mind to Matter	41
Chapter 6: The Sacred Expanse of the Akashic Field	50
Chapter 7: The Enigmatic Quantum Consciousness	59
Chapter 8: The Infinite Expanse of Possibility	67
Chapter 9: The Sacred Geometry of the Universe	75
Chapter 10: The Quantum Heart: Weaving the Threads of Science and Spirituality	85
Chapter 11: The Journey Within- Exploring Inner Realms Through Quantum Consciousness	93
Chapter 12: The Mystical Quantum: Beyond the Material World	101

Chapter 13: The Sacred Echo: Resonating with the Divine Through Quantum Understanding	110
Chapter 14: The Quantum Pilgrimage: A Spiritual Quest Through Science	118
Chapter 15: The Divine Blueprint: Understanding Life's Purpose Through Quantum Principles	127
Chapter 16: The Alchemy of Quantum and Spirituality	135
Chapter 17: The Sacred Observer: The Power of Awareness in Quantum and Spiritual Realms	143
Chapter 18: The Quantum Key: Unlocking the Secrets of the Universe and the Soul	151
Chapter 19: The Sacred Wave: Riding the Quantum Currents of Life	160
Chapter 20: The Quantum Awakening: A Call to Spiritual Consciousness	167
Chapter 21: The Quantum Rituals: Sacred Practices for Modern Times	174
Chapter 22: The Quantum Mindfulness: Meditation and the Sacred Now	183
Chapter 23: The Sacred Quantum Relationships: Love in the Quantum Field	191
Chapter 24: The Quantum Path of Compassion	200
Chapter 25: The Sacred Art of Quantum Creation	208
Chapter 26: The Quantum Evolution: A New Vision for Humanity	215
Chapter 27: The Quantum Legacy: Passing the Torch to Future Generations	224
Chapter 28: The Sacred Symphony: Harmonizing	232

Science and Spirit in the World

Chapter 29: The Quantum Homecoming: Returning to the Source — 241

Chapter 30: The Sacred Quantum Revelation: A Final Reflection — 249

Epilogue: The Endless Dance of Quantum and Spirit — 256

Acknowledgements — 261

Copyright Information — 263

Disclaimer — 264

THE JOURNEY OF QUANTUM SPIRITUALITY

Dr Bhaskar Bora

DR BHASKAR BORA

QUANTUM SPIRITUALITY

A PERSONAL NOTE FROM THE AUTHOR

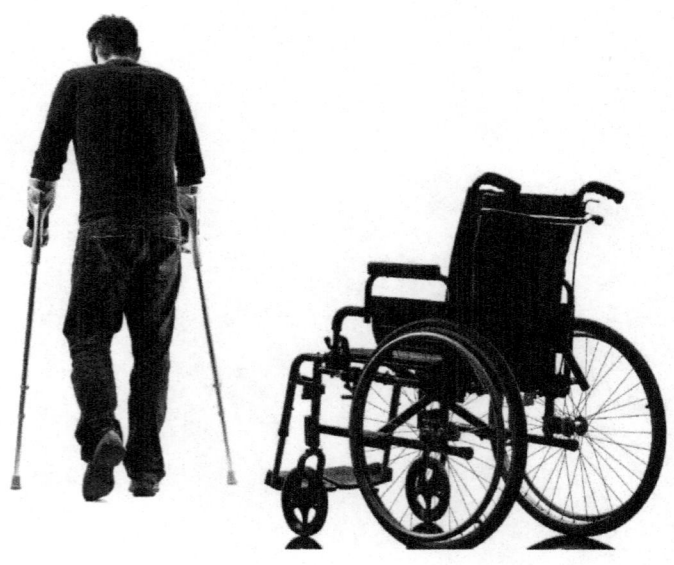

My journey, once marked by certainty and driven by purpose, has transformed in ways I could never have anticipated. It is no longer about grand achievements or the pursuit of external success, but about the quiet, tender moments that reveal the true essence of life—moments of love, care, and presence. What you hold in your hands is not just a collection of words, but a testament to resilience, a story woven from the delicate threads of struggle, acceptance, and ultimately, renewal.

There was a time when my life flowed with the grace of a symphony, every note in perfect harmony. As a doctor, my days were filled with the pulse of life itself—offering hope, easing suffering, and healing with steady hands. The white coat I wore wasn't just a symbol of my profession; it embodied my very identity; an outward reflection of the healer I believed I was destined to be. The lives I touched, the people I helped—it all gave profound meaning to my existence.

But life, in its mysterious and unpredictable ways, had other plans. In one swift, unforeseen moment, the world I knew unravelled. First came the spinal cord injury, stripping away the physical strength I had relied upon. Then, the shadow of cancer darkened the horizon, a stark reminder of life's fragility. The world of medicine, where I once found so much joy and purpose, suddenly slipped away, leaving a vast emptiness in its wake—a silence where once there had been meaning.

Gone were the bustling corridors of the hospital, replaced by the quiet solitude of my home. No longer a "Doctor," I found myself standing at the edge of an uncertain future, my hands—once so steady with the knowledge of healing—trembling with questions I wasn't ready to face. Without the title, without the work that had defined me for so long, who was I? What was left of me when everything I had known was no longer within reach?

In that silence, in the stillness of a life interrupted, I began to uncover something unexpected. The role of a disabled husband and father, once a distant concept, became my new reality—one that held unexpected grace.

What began as an effort to nurture my relationships, to find solace in this new world, slowly evolved into a profound inward journey.

I found healing in the spiritual—a rhythm of meditation, reading, and reflection that allowed me to rediscover the parts of myself I thought were lost. As I immersed myself in books, audiobooks, and hours of research, I began to understand that this new chapter of my life was not an ending, but a rebirth. The solitude of these years, the quiet hours of writing and reflection, gave birth to the very pages you hold in your hands now.
It is with deep gratitude that I share these words with you, knowing that they carry with them not just knowledge, but a piece of my soul. I hope that these reflections and insights offer you a fresh perspective on life and perhaps some nourishment for your own journey.

We cannot control what the universe throws at us, but how we react to those curveballs defines who we are and what we make of our lives.

CHAPTER 1: THE ETERNAL DANCE OF THE QUANTUM AND THE DIVINE

In the beginning, when the cosmos was but a breath within the void, a delicate dance began—a dance of light and shadow, of energy and matter, of the seen and the unseen. This dance, an eternal waltz, continues to weave the very fabric of our reality, a dance that marries the precision of science with the transcendence of the sacred. It is within this intricate interplay that the profound mysteries of existence unfold—the dance of the quantum and the divine.

The Quantum Symphony

In the quantum realm, paradox reigns, where particles exist not as fixed entities but as whispers of potential, undefined until observed. Here, certainty melts into probability, and the act of observation itself becomes an act of creation, shaping reality in a way that is both precise and poetic. Imagine the delicate ballet of these particles—their subtle vibrations, their fleeting collisions, their silent pirouettes through the void. Each particle is a note in the cosmic symphony, moving in harmony with the others, crafting a melody that is as fleeting as it is eternal. This symphony, unbound by time and space, exists in a superposition where all possibilities coalesce.

Yet, this quantum symphony transcends mere scientific curiosity; it reflects a deeper, sacred reality. It offers a glimpse into the divine architecture that underpins all of existence, a window into the infinite wisdom that guides the cosmos. To delve into the quantum is to brush against the sacred, to feel the pulse of creation resonating through the void.

The Sacred Mirror

In the ancient wisdom of the East, sages spoke of a reality beyond the material, a reality perceived not by the eyes but by the soul's inner vision. They spoke of the Tao, the ineffable essence that courses through all things, birthing the universe and giving it form. The Tao is the rhythm of the cosmos, the dance of the divine.

Modern quantum physics, in its pursuit of the fundamental nature of reality, has inadvertently echoed this ancient wisdom. The principles that govern the quantum realm—uncertainty, wave-particle duality, entanglement—are more than just scientific phenomena; they are reflections of the sacred, whispers of the Tao.

Consider wave-particle duality, where entities like

electrons exhibit both particle-like and wave-like properties. In the quantum world, an electron is both wave and particle, suspended in superposition until the moment of observation. This duality is not a contradiction but a manifestation of the underlying unity of all things, a reminder that the material and the mystical are not separate but two facets of the same cosmic reality.

The Tao, too, is a dance of opposites—yin and yang, light and dark, form and formlessness. The harmony of the cosmos arises from the unity of these opposites. Just as the electron can be both wave and particle, so the Tao is both the manifest and the unmanifest, the known and the unknowable. In this way, the quantum realm mirrors the sacred, reflecting the deeper truths that have been intuited by mystics for millennia.

The Observer and the Observed

In the quantum domain, the observer holds a pivotal role, collapsing the wave function and transforming potential into reality. This act of observation is not passive; it is an act of creation, a dance between the observer and the observed.

This concept is deeply rooted in spiritual traditions. Many mystical teachings regard perception as a sacred act, one that shapes and defines reality. Ancient sages taught that reality is not fixed but fluid, moulded by the consciousness that perceives it. The world, they said, reflects the mind, a mirror that reveals the state of the observer's soul.

In this light, the quantum observer is not merely a

scientist peering through an instrument but a participant in the cosmic dance of creation. The act of observation is a moment of communion with the divine, where the material and the mystical converge.

Eastern scriptures speak of the unity of the observer and the observed, of the seer and the seen. They teach that the division between self and other, between subject and object, is an illusion—a veil that obscures the true nature of reality. In the quantum world, this unity is mirrored in the phenomenon of entanglement, where particles that have once interacted remain connected, their states influencing each other instantaneously, regardless of distance. This entanglement is a testament to the interconnectedness of all things, a reflection of the sacred web of life.

The Quantum Leap

The quantum realm is one of leaps and bounds, of sudden shifts and unexpected transformations. Here, particles tunnel through barriers, energy levels shift in discrete steps, and reality itself seems to leap from one state to another. This quantum leap is not merely a physical phenomenon but a metaphor for the spiritual journey.

On the spiritual path, moments of profound transformation occur—moments when the soul leaps into the unknown, transcending the ego and ascending to higher states of consciousness. These moments of spiritual awakening are akin to the quantum leap, sudden and transformative, leading to new vistas of understanding.

Ancient texts describe these leaps as enlightenment, the

moment when the veil lifts and the true nature of reality is revealed. In the quantum world, the leap happens when a particle shifts from one energy level to another without traversing the space in between—a sudden, discontinuous change, a moment of transformation that defies the logic of the material world.

The quantum leap reminds us that reality is not linear, that change does not always unfold gradually but can occur in an instant, in a flash of insight, in a moment of grace. It is a reminder that the journey toward the sacred is not a step-by-step progression but a series of leaps into the unknown, guided by the soul's light.

The Dance of the Sacred and the Scientific

As we venture deeper into the mysteries of the quantum realm, we find ourselves drawn into a dance that transcends the boundaries of science and spirituality. This dance invites us to abandon our preconceptions, to open our minds and hearts to the infinite possibilities that lie beyond the material world.

In this dance, the scientific and the sacred are not separate but intertwined, moving together in a harmonious rhythm that reflects the unity of all things. The principles of quantum physics—uncertainty, wave-particle duality, entanglement—are not merely abstract concepts but reflections of the deeper truths known to mystics and sages for millennia.

The uncertainty principle, which tells us that the position and momentum of a particle cannot both be precisely known, reminds us of the limits of human knowledge and the mystery that lies at the heart of reality. It calls us to humility, to recognize that some aspects of the universe remain beyond our understanding, that the sacred cannot be fully comprehended by the mind alone.

Wave-particle duality, which reveals that particles can exhibit both wave-like and particle-like properties, reflects the unity of opposites, the dance between the material and the mystical. It reminds us that reality is fluid, that the sacred permeates both the visible and the invisible.

Entanglement, where particles remain connected across vast distances, reflects the interconnectedness of all things. It reminds us that we are all part of the same sacred web of life, that the divisions between self and other, between science and spirituality, are mere illusions.

In this dance of the quantum and the sacred, we are invited to transcend the dualities that divide us, to enter into a state of unity where the scientific and the spiritual are one. We are invited to see the world not as a collection of separate parts but as a harmonious whole, where every particle, every wave, every moment reflects the divine.

The Sacred Journey

As we stand at the threshold of this sacred journey, we prepare to delve into the heart of the quantum realm, where the mysteries of science and spirituality converge. This journey requires us to let go of our preconceptions, to open ourselves to the unknown, to embrace the paradoxes that lie at the heart of reality.

This journey is not merely an intellectual pursuit but

a spiritual quest, a search for the deeper truths that underlie the material world. It invites us to perceive the sacred in the ordinary, to recognize the divine in the dance of particles and waves.

As we embark on this journey, let us remember that the quantum world is not separate from us but a reflection of our inner reality. The dance of the quantum and the sacred is a dance that unfolds within us, inviting us to awaken to the deeper dimensions of our being, to enter into communion with the divine.

In this dance, we are both the observer and the observed, the dancer and the dance. We are part of the cosmic symphony, a note in the melody of creation, a wave in the ocean of existence. As we move through this sacred dance, we are invited to release our fears, to embrace the mystery, to surrender to the flow of the Tao, and to find our place in the infinite dance of the quantum and the sacred.

The dance of the quantum and the sacred is a journey into the heart of reality, where science and spirituality converge. It is a journey that invites us to see the world with new eyes, to recognize the divine in the interplay of particles and waves, and to embrace the profound mystery of existence. As we continue this journey in the chapters to come, we will explore the deeper truths that lie at the intersection of science and the sacred and discover the boundless wisdom that awaits us in the quantum realm.

CHAPTER 2: THE CELESTIAL TAPESTRY OF EXISTENCE

In the infinite expanse of the cosmos, where galaxies pirouette like ethereal wraiths and stars shimmer as ancient sentinels, there lies an invisible lattice—a vast, intricate nexus that binds every particle, every being, every thought. This is the Divine Matrix, the celestial loom that undergirds the very essence of reality, interlacing the threads of existence into a coherent and harmonious symphony. It is the subtle, unseen force that fuses the universe in oneness, a transcendent and empirical phenomenon that surpasses the confines of our perception, beckoning us to witness the profound interconnectedness of all life.

The Celestial Weave

To fathom the Divine Matrix, one must first perceive

the universe as an expansive tapestry, intricately woven with the filaments of energy and consciousness. Every atom, every molecule, every quantum entity is a strand in this celestial weave, contributing to the grand design of existence. The ancients spoke of the web of life, a delicate balance connecting all living beings. In modernity, quantum physics unveils this as a scientific reality—an interconnected reality where the actions of a single particle can reverberate across the cosmos, shaping the entire tapestry.

Envision the universe as an enormous, multidimensional loom, where the warp and weft of energy and matter intertwine in an elaborate mosaic. This pattern is far from arbitrary; it is guided by the invisible hand of the Divine Matrix, ensuring that every thread is meticulously placed, creating a design that is both intricate and sublime. The Divine Matrix is the blueprint of the cosmos, the underlying structure that gives form to the formless and order to the chaos. It is the sacred geometry that sculpts reality, the cosmic architecture that orchestrates the flow of energy and the manifestation of matter.

Within this celestial weave, nothing exists in solitude. Every particle is intertwined with every other, every thought with every other thought, every soul with every other soul. This interconnectedness transcends mere philosophy; it is a scientific verity, revealed through the principles of quantum entanglement and nonlocality. These principles reveal that distance is an illusion, separation a fallacy, and that the universe operates as a unified whole, where all is in perpetual communion.

Quantum Entanglement: The Filaments of Unity

Quantum entanglement stands as one of the most enigmatic discoveries of modern science, a phenomenon that defies conventional understanding of space and time. When two particles become entangled, their states become inextricably linked, such that the state of one particle instantaneously influences the state of the other, regardless of the distance between them. This connection transcends the speed of light, the vastness of space; it is immediate, inexplicable, transcending the physical plane.

This phenomenon intimates that, at a fundamental level, the universe is profoundly interconnected, that the boundaries we perceive between objects and beings are not as impermeable as they seem. The entangled particles are like twin dancers moving in flawless synchrony, their movements mirroring each other across the void. They are two notes in a cosmic symphony, resonating in harmony despite the chasm that separates them.

The implications of quantum entanglement extend far beyond the microcosm of particles. They suggest a deeper truth—that all entities in the universe are entangled, that we are all threads in a vast, interconnected tapestry. Our thoughts, emotions, and actions are not solitary occurrences; they are strands within the Divine Matrix, influencing and being influenced by the greater whole. The ancient wisdom that teaches "we are all one" reverberates through the revelations of quantum physics, revealing that our interconnectedness is not merely spiritual dogma but a scientific certainty.

The Divine Matrix: A Celestial Consciousness

If the Divine Matrix is the web that connects all things,

then consciousness is the force that weaves this web. The universe is not a lifeless, mechanical construct governed by impersonal laws; it is a living, breathing organism, infused with consciousness at every tier. This consciousness is the quintessence of the Divine Matrix, the intelligence that choreographs the dance of particles, the creativity that gives birth to galaxies, the love that binds all in unity.

Consciousness is not confined to human beings or even to living organisms; it permeates the entire cosmos. It is the ground of being, the wellspring from which all things emerge. The Divine Matrix is not merely a physical framework; it is a field of consciousness, a vast ocean of awareness in which all forms of life are submerged. This field is the medium through which information flows, through which thoughts and intentions are transmitted, through which the universe expresses its essence.

In this conception, the Divine Matrix is both the loom and the weaver, the structure and the substance, the container and the contained. It is the sacred space where consciousness and matter converge, where the physical and the metaphysical intersect. It is the matrix of all possibilities, the quantum field in which all potential realities reside. Through the Divine Matrix, consciousness crafts reality, shaping the world according to its desires and intentions.

The Alchemy of Intention

One of the most profound implications of the Divine Matrix is the power of intention. If the universe is a sentient entity, if reality is moulded by the flow of consciousness, then our thoughts and intentions possess the power to influence the world around us. The Divine Matrix responds to our consciousness, to our beliefs, to our desires. It is the mirror of the soul, reflecting the reality we project into it.

In ancient teachings, it is said that the mind shapes reality, that the world reflects our inner state. Contemporary science echoes this wisdom, demonstrating that the observer plays a crucial role in the formation of reality. The act of observation collapses the wave function, transforming a field of potential into a concrete reality. Our thoughts, beliefs, and intentions are the instruments through which we shape the world, the threads with which we weave the fabric of our lives.

In the Divine Matrix, nothing is immutable, nothing is preordained. Reality is fluid, malleable, subject to the influence of consciousness. This is the essence of creation, the secret of manifestation. By aligning our intentions with the flow of the Divine Matrix, we can co-create reality, bringing forth the life we envision, the world we desire.

The power of intention is not confined to the individual; it extends to the collective consciousness, to the shared intentions of humanity. The Divine Matrix is the medium through which collective intentions manifest, through which the dreams and aspirations of a species are realized. The world we inhabit reflects our collective consciousness, a mirror of our shared beliefs and desires. By altering our collective intentions, we can reshape the world.

The Sacred Geometry of the Matrix

The Divine Matrix is not a haphazard, chaotic web; it is a structure of exquisite order and harmony, governed by the principles of sacred geometry. Sacred geometry is the study of the patterns and shapes that form the bedrock of the universe, the blueprints of creation. From the spiral of galaxies to the symmetry of a snowflake, sacred geometry is the language of the Divine Matrix, the code through which reality is inscribed.

The shapes and patterns of sacred geometry are not arbitrary; they are the expressions of the fundamental principles that govern the cosmos. They are the fingerprints of the divine, the signatures of the consciousness that sculpts reality. The Flower of Life, the Golden Ratio, the Platonic solids—these are not merely mathematical constructs; they are the building blocks of the Divine Matrix, the forms through which consciousness manifests.

Through the lens of sacred geometry, we can perceive the Divine Matrix as a living, dynamic structure, a web of energy and consciousness in perpetual evolution, in constant creation. It is a reminder that the universe is not static but alive, that reality is not fixed but fluid. It is an invitation to align ourselves with the flow of the Divine Matrix, to attune to the sacred patterns that shape reality, to become conscious co-creators of the world.

The Heart of the Matrix: Love as the Unifying Force

At the core of the Divine Matrix lies a force more potent than any physical law, more primordial than any scientific principle. This force is love, the unifying energy that binds the universe together. Love is the essence of the Divine Matrix, the glue that holds the web of reality in place, the force that animates the dance of creation.

In the spiritual traditions of the world, love is regarded as the highest expression of the divine, the ultimate truth that transcends all dualities. It is the force that connects all beings, that reconciles all opposites, that heals all fractures. In the Divine Matrix, love is the thread that weaves the fabric of reality, the current that flows through the web of life, connecting every particle, every being, every thought.

Modern science is beginning to recognize love's role as a unifying force, not just in the realm of human relationships but in the very structure of the cosmos. Studies in quantum physics, neuroscience, and psychology are uncovering the profound influence of love on the mind, the body, and the world. Love is not merely an emotion; it is a state of consciousness, a frequency that resonates with the core of the Divine Matrix.

In the Divine Matrix, love is the key to creation, the force that shapes reality. When we align our intentions with the frequency of love, we access the creative power of the universe, the force that shapes reality according to the highest good. Love is the harmonizing force that brings order to chaos, the healing force that mends the broken, the creative force that births the new.

To live in harmony with the Divine Matrix is to live in a state of love, to honour the interconnectedness of all things, to perceive the sacredness of life. It is to view the world through the heart's eyes, to feel the pulse of the universe in every beat of our own. It is to become an active participant in the dance of creation, a co-weaver of reality, a thread in the web of life.

The Sacred Summons

As we draw this chapter to a close, we are beckoned to awaken to the reality of the Divine Matrix, to perceive the unseen web that binds us all. This web is not merely a scientific curiosity; it is a spiritual truth, a reminder that we are integral parts of a greater whole, that our lives are interwoven with the lives of others, that our actions send ripples through the cosmos.

The Divine Matrix invites us to step into our roles as conscious creators, to align our intentions with the cosmic flow, to weave our threads into the fabric of reality. It calls us to dwell in love, to honour the interconnectedness of all things, to discern the sacred in the mundane, the divine in the ordinary.

In the Divine Matrix, we are not isolated entities but essential strands in a cosmic tapestry. We are notes in the symphony of creation, dancers in the universal ballet. And as we traverse this sacred dance, we are reminded that we are not separate from the world but intricately connected to it in ways both profound and mysterious.

The Divine Matrix is the unseen web of existence, the celestial lattice that binds all life and consciousness. It reflects the sacred, a reminder that we are all part of a greater whole, that our lives are intertwined with the lives of others, that our actions send ripples across the cosmos. As we continue our journey into the heart of quantum spirituality, let this awareness guide us in the dance of life.

The Divine Matrix transcends mere scientific concept;

it is a spiritual reality that connects all things. By understanding and aligning with this unseen web, we can tap into the profound power of intention, love, and consciousness to shape our reality and live in harmony with the cosmos. As we explore the deeper truths of quantum spirituality, we are invited to perceive the world with new vision, to acknowledge our interconnectedness, and to participate in the dance of creation with hearts full of love and minds open to the infinite possibilities within the Divine Matrix.

CHAPTER 3: THE HOLOGRAPHIC NATURE OF THE UNIVERSE

In the silent void where the universe began, where time had yet to stretch its fingers and space was but a thought in the mind of the cosmos, there lay a secret—a secret encoded in the very fabric of reality, a secret that would one day be glimpsed through the lens of science and the eyes of the mystic alike. This secret is the holographic nature of the universe, a profound and awe-inspiring truth that challenges our understanding of reality and invites us to reconsider our spiritual place within the cosmos.

The Holographic Revelation

Imagine holding a small fragment of a hologram, a seemingly insignificant piece of a larger picture. If you shine a light through this fragment, you don't merely see a portion of the image—you see the entire picture, albeit in a smaller, less detailed form. Every piece of a hologram contains the whole; each part mirrors the entirety. This principle, while a marvel of optical physics, is also a profound metaphor for the nature of the universe itself.

The idea that the universe operates as a hologram was once relegated to the realms of science fiction and speculative thought. Yet, as our understanding of quantum physics deepens, this concept has gained scientific traction, challenging the very foundations of what we perceive as reality. The universe, it seems, is not a collection of separate, independent objects, but a vast, interconnected web where every part contains the whole.

In this holographic universe, each fragment of reality—every atom, every cell, every individual consciousness—contains within it the entirety of the cosmos. This is not merely a poetic notion; it reflects the underlying structure of the universe, a structure that is far more interconnected and interdependent than our everyday experience suggests.

The Illusion of Separation

The holographic nature of the universe offers a radical departure from the traditional view of reality as a collection of distinct and separate entities. In our everyday experience, we perceive the world as composed of individual objects, each existing independently of the others. We see ourselves as separate from the world around us, distinct from the people we interact with, isolated in our own subjective experience.

But if the universe is indeed holographic, this perception

of separation is an illusion—a convincing illusion, to be sure, but an illusion, nonetheless. In reality, there are no true boundaries, no real divisions. The apparent separateness of objects and beings is a consequence of the way we perceive the world, not a reflection of the underlying reality.

The implications of this are profound. If each part of the universe contains the whole, then everything is interconnected in a way that transcends our conventional understanding. The boundary between self and other, between subject and object, between mind and matter, begins to dissolve. We are not isolated individuals but integral parts of a cosmic whole, connected to everything and everyone around us in ways that are both subtle and profound.

This realization invites us to rethink our relationship with the world, with each other, and with ourselves. It calls us to recognize the inherent unity of all things, to see the divine in the mundane, the infinite in the finite. It invites us to transcend the illusion of separation and to embrace a more holistic, interconnected view of reality.

The Mirror of the Mind

The holographic nature of the universe is not limited to the physical world; it extends into the realm of consciousness as well. Just as every part of a hologram contains the whole image, so too does each individual consciousness contain the entirety of the cosmos. This idea is echoed in the mystical traditions of the world, which teach that the microcosm reflects the macrocosm, that the inner world of the mind mirrors the outer world of the universe.

In this view, the mind is not a mere byproduct of the brain, nor is it confined to the physical body. The mind is a holographic entity, a reflection of the cosmic consciousness that pervades the universe. It is a window through which the universe perceives itself, a microcosm that contains within it the totality of existence.

The implications of this are staggering. If the mind is indeed a hologram of the universe, then our thoughts, feelings, and perceptions are not isolated events, but reflections of the greater whole. Our consciousness is not separate from the world; it is a part of the world, a reflection of the divine consciousness that underlies all of reality.

This understanding challenges the conventional view of consciousness as something that is created by the brain and confined to the individual. Instead, it suggests that consciousness is a fundamental aspect of the universe, an intrinsic part of the fabric of reality. It invites us to see our minds not as isolated entities, but as integral parts of the cosmic consciousness, connected to everything and everyone around us.

The Sacred Implications

The holographic nature of the universe has profound spiritual implications. If every part contains the whole, then every aspect of existence is sacred, every moment is divine, every being reflects the cosmic consciousness. This understanding invites us to see the world through new eyes, to recognize the sacred in the ordinary, to find the divine in the mundane.

In many spiritual traditions, the concept of the

holographic universe is expressed in terms of unity and interconnectedness. The mystics speak of the oneness of all things, the interconnectedness of all life, the unity of the self and the divine. These teachings, once considered esoteric and abstract, find a new resonance in the light of the holographic universe. They are not merely metaphors or symbols; they are reflections of the underlying structure of reality.

This understanding calls us to live in a way that honours the interconnectedness of all things. It invites us to see the world as a reflection of the divine, to treat every being with respect and compassion, to recognize the inherent worth and dignity of every individual. It challenges us to transcend the illusion of separation and to embrace a more holistic, inclusive view of life.

In this view, spirituality is not something that is separate from everyday life; it is the very essence of life itself. Every action, every thought, every interaction reflects the greater whole, a part of the cosmic dance. The sacred is not something that is confined to religious rituals or spiritual practices; it is present in every moment, in every breath, in every heartbeat.

The Power of Reflection

If the universe is holographic, then we are constantly reflecting and being reflected by the world around us. Our thoughts and intentions are not isolated events; they are waves in the cosmic ocean, ripples that extend outwards, influencing the whole. The universe responds to our consciousness, reflecting back to us the reality we project into it.

This understanding gives us a profound responsibility. If our consciousness reflects the cosmic consciousness, then our thoughts and intentions have the power to shape reality. We are not passive observers in the holographic universe; we are active participants, co-creators of the world we experience.

This realization invites us to cultivate a deeper awareness of our thoughts and intentions, to recognize the power we have to influence the world around us. It challenges us to live with greater mindfulness, to be conscious of the energy we project into the universe, to align our intentions with the greater good.

Meditation, prayer, and other spiritual practices are not merely ways to connect with the divine; they are ways to shape reality, to influence the holographic field in which we live. By aligning our consciousness with the divine, we can create a reality that reflects the highest ideals of love, compassion, and unity.

The Infinite Within

One of the most profound aspects of the holographic universe is the idea that the infinite is contained within the finite, that the entirety of the cosmos is present in every particle, every moment, every being. This understanding challenges our conventional notions of space and time, inviting us to see the universe as a boundless, infinite reality that is present in every aspect of existence.

This idea is reflected in the mystical traditions of the world, which teach that the divine is present in all things, that the infinite is contained within the finite, that the sacred is present in the ordinary. These teachings, once considered abstract and esoteric, find a new resonance in the light of the holographic universe. They are not merely metaphors or symbols; they are reflections of the underlying structure of reality.

This understanding invites us to see the infinite in the finite, to recognize the divine in the ordinary, to find the sacred in the mundane. It challenges us to transcend our limited perspective and to embrace a more expansive, holistic view of reality.

Every moment is an opportunity to connect with the infinite, to touch the divine, to experience the sacred. The infinite is not something that is distant or inaccessible; it is present in every breath, in every heartbeat, in every moment of our lives.

The Journey Inward

The holographic nature of the universe invites us on a journey inward, a journey to explore the depths of our own consciousness, to discover the infinite within ourselves. This journey is not merely a spiritual quest; it is a scientific exploration, a quest to understand the true nature of reality and our place within it.

As we journey inward, we discover that the boundaries between self and other, between mind and matter, between the finite and the infinite, begin to dissolve. We begin to see ourselves not as isolated individuals, but as integral parts of the cosmic whole, connected to everything and everyone around us.

This journey invites us to explore the depths of our own consciousness, to discover the infinite within ourselves, to recognize the divine in the mirror of the mind. It challenges us to transcend the illusion of separation and to embrace a more holistic, interconnected view of reality.

In this journey, we discover that the universe is not a collection of separate, independent objects, but a vast, interconnected web where every part contains the whole. We discover that our consciousness is not separate from the world, but a reflection of the cosmic consciousness that pervades the universe. We discover that the sacred is not something that is distant or inaccessible, but present in every moment, in every breath, in every heartbeat.

The Holographic Dance

As we conclude this chapter, we find ourselves standing on the threshold of a new understanding of reality, a new awareness of our place within the universe. The holographic nature of the universe invites us to see the world through new eyes, to recognize the interconnectedness of all things, to find the sacred in the ordinary, the infinite in the finite.

This understanding challenges us to live with greater awareness, to recognize the power we have to shape reality, to align our consciousness with the divine. It invites us to participate in the holographic dance, to become conscious co-creators of the world we experience.

The holographic universe is not just a scientific concept; it is a spiritual reality, a reflection of the underlying structure of existence. It invites us to see the world as a reflection of the divine, to recognize the interconnectedness of all things, to find the sacred in the ordinary, the infinite in the finite.

As we continue our journey into the heart of quantum spirituality, let us carry this awareness with us, and let it guide us in the dance of life. Let us see the world as a reflection of the divine, as a hologram where every part contains the whole. Let us recognize the infinite within ourselves and let us live in a way that honours the interconnectedness of all things.

The holographic nature of the universe challenges our conventional understanding of reality, inviting us to see the world as an interconnected web where every part contains the whole. This understanding has profound spiritual implications, calling us to recognize the sacred in the ordinary, the infinite in the finite, and to live in a way that honours the interconnectedness of all things. As we explore the deeper truths of quantum spirituality, we are invited to participate in the holographic dance, to become conscious co-creators of the world we experience, and to find the divine in every aspect of existence.

CHAPTER 4: THE QUANTUM MIND: CONSCIOUSNESS AS THE BEDROCK OF EXISTENCE

In the serene alcoves of the mind, where thoughts unfurl like ripples upon a placid lake, there lies a truth as ancient as time—a truth murmured by mystics, pondered by philosophers, and now unravelled by scientists. This truth speaks to the primacy of consciousness, a profound realization that the mind, rather than matter, is the foundational essence of the cosmos. In this chapter, we explore the radical idea that consciousness is not a mere byproduct of the brain, but the very bedrock of existence, the wellspring from which all reality emerges.

The Ascendancy of Consciousness

For millennia, the reigning paradigm in science has been materialism—the conviction that matter is the cornerstone of the universe, with consciousness arising as a secondary effect of intricate material processes within the brain. This perspective has permeated modern thought, leading us to perceive the world as a collection of physical entities, governed by the unyielding laws of physics, with consciousness relegated to a subordinate, almost incidental role.

Yet, as we delve into the enigma of quantum physics, this materialistic worldview begins to disintegrate. Quantum mechanics unveils a cosmos far more enigmatic and intertwined than we ever imagined, a cosmos where the observer's gaze is intrinsic to the shaping of reality, where consciousness appears to be interwoven with the very fabric of existence.

The question thus arises: What if consciousness is not a mere epiphenomenon of matter, but the fundamental reality from which matter itself unfurls? What if the mind is not a passive witness to the world, but an active architect in the creation of reality? This is the revolutionary premise advanced by thinkers like Amit Goswami, who propose that consciousness, not matter, is the true ground of being.

In this view, the universe is not a soulless machine, grinding away according to impersonal laws, but a sentient, conscious entity, sculpted by the intentions and perceptions of conscious beings. Reality is not an independent construct, existing apart from the mind; it is a co-creation, a fluid and dynamic experience shaped by the consciousness that perceives it.

The Quantum Observer

At the core of quantum mechanics lies the enigma of the observer—the notion that the mere act of observation influences the outcome of an experiment. In the renowned double-slit experiment, for instance, particles like electrons behave as waves when unobserved, creating an interference pattern on a screen. However, when these particles are observed, they adopt a particulate nature, forming discrete points. The act of observation alters the particles' behaviour, collapsing their wave-like potential into a concrete reality.

This phenomenon, known as the "observer effect," challenges the traditional notion of an objective, independent reality. It suggests that reality does not exist "out there," separate from the observer, but is deeply intertwined with the consciousness of the observer. In essence, the mind plays a central role in the creation of reality.

This concept carries profound implications for our understanding of the universe. It implies that consciousness is not a passive spectator of reality, but an active participant in its creation. The universe is not a fixed, preordained structure but a dynamic, evolving process, continuously shaped by the consciousness that perceives it.

In this perspective, the mind is not confined to the brain or the body; it is a vast field of consciousness that interacts with the quantum field, co-creating the reality we experience. The observer and the observed are not distinct entities but two facets of a unified reality, intimately connected and interdependent. Observation is not a mere reception of data, but a creative act, a participation in the ongoing genesis of the universe.

Consciousness and the Quantum Field

If consciousness is the ground of being, it must be intrinsically connected to the quantum field—the primordial field of potential that gives birth to the material world. The quantum field is a realm of boundless possibilities, where particles exist as waves of potentiality, becoming definite only through observation. It is a field of pure potential, an ocean of possibilities that consciousness can mould into tangible reality.

In this view, the quantum field is not distinct from consciousness; it is an extension of it, a field of potential responsive to the intentions and perceptions of the mind. The mind, in turn, is not limited to the confines of the brain or the body; it is a field of consciousness that transcends the physical, interacting with the quantum field to shape reality.

This understanding challenges the conventional view of the mind as a mere product of the brain. Instead, it suggests that the brain is a receiver or conduit of consciousness, a biological interface that enables the mind to interact with the physical world. The brain does not generate consciousness; it processes and channels it, translating the infinite potential of the quantum field into the finite experience of reality.

This view of consciousness as the bedrock of existence is bolstered by an expanding body of scientific evidence, including studies on near-death experiences, out-of-body experiences, and other phenomena that hint at consciousness existing independently of the body. These experiences challenge the materialistic conception of consciousness and suggest that the mind is a fundamental facet of reality, not a mere byproduct of neural processes.

The Creative Power of Consciousness

If consciousness is the bedrock of existence, then it follows that the mind possesses the power to shape reality. This idea is not novel; it is a cornerstone of many spiritual traditions, which teach that the mind crafts reality, that thoughts and intentions possess the power to manifest in the physical world. Modern science, through the lens of quantum mechanics, is beginning to acknowledge the veracity of this ancient wisdom.

In the quantum realm, reality is not rigid; it is a field of potential that can be shaped by consciousness. The act of observation collapses the wave function, transforming potential into actuality, possibility into reality. This process is not confined to particles in a laboratory; it is a universal principle that governs all aspects of existence. Our thoughts, our beliefs, our intentions—all possess the power to mould the reality we experience.

This understanding calls us to assume responsibility for the reality we create. It challenges us to become conscious creators of our lives, to recognize the power we wield in shaping our world through the power of our minds. It invites us to cultivate a deeper awareness of our thoughts and intentions and to align our consciousness with the highest ideals of love, compassion, and unity.

In this light, spiritual practices such as meditation, prayer, and visualization are not merely ways to connect with the divine; they are potent tools for shaping reality. By aligning our consciousness with the quantum field, we can create a reality that reflects our highest aspirations, a world in harmony with the divine.

The Path to Spiritual Awakening

The recognition that consciousness is the bedrock of existence is not just an intellectual insight; it is a pathway to spiritual awakening. It beckons us to transcend the illusion of separation, to perceive the unity of all things, to discern the divine within the mirror of the mind. It challenges us to awaken to our true nature as conscious beings, co-creators of reality, and active participants in the ongoing creation of the universe.

This journey toward spiritual awakening is not about retreating from the world; it is about engaging with the world in a deeper, more meaningful way. It is about recognizing the interconnectedness of all existence, the unity of mind and matter, the symphony of the physical and the spiritual. It is about perceiving the world as a reflection of the divine, a manifestation of consciousness, a sacred dance of creation.

In this quest for awakening, we are invited to delve into the depths of our consciousness, to uncover the infinite potential within, to align our minds with the divine consciousness that permeates the cosmos. We are invited to become conscious participants in the creation of reality, to live in harmony with the quantum field, and to manifest a world that embodies the highest ideals of love, compassion, and unity.

This path to awakening is not about attaining some distant goal; it is about awakening to the truth of our being, here and now. It is about recognizing that we are not separate from the cosmos but integral to it, that our consciousness is not confined to the brain or body but is a field of potential that transcends the physical. It is about perceiving the divine in every moment, the sacred in the mundane, the infinite in the finite.

The Unity of Mind and Matter

One of the most profound revelations of the quantum mind is the unity of mind and matter. In the traditional materialistic worldview, mind and matter are seen as distinct and separate—mind as a product of the brain, and matter as the fundamental substance of the cosmos. But if consciousness is the bedrock of existence, then mind and matter are not separate; they are two expressions of the same reality.

In this view, matter is not inert or lifeless; it is a manifestation of consciousness, a reflection of the quantum field. The physical world is not detached from the mind; it is a creation of the mind, sculpted by the intentions and perceptions of consciousness. The mind and the world are not two separate entities but a unified whole, interconnected and interdependent.

This understanding challenges the dualism that has dominated Western thought for centuries—the division between mind and matter, subject and object, self and other. It invites us to transcend this dualism, to perceive the unity of all things, to acknowledge the interconnectedness of mind and matter, consciousness and the physical world.

In this light, the universe is not a collection of isolated, independent objects, but an immense, interconnected web of consciousness and matter, where every part is linked to every other, where mind and matter dance together in the act of creation. The physical world is not separate from consciousness; it reflects it, a manifestation of the quantum field, a mirror of the divine.

The Sacred Odyssey

As we conclude this chapter, we find ourselves standing on the threshold of a sacred odyssey—a journey into the heart of the quantum mind, where consciousness and the physical world are intertwined in the dance of creation. This odyssey invites us to awaken to the truth of our existence, to recognize the power of consciousness to shape reality, to perceive the world as a reflection of the divine.

The quantum mind is not merely a scientific concept; it is a spiritual reality, a reflection of the cosmos's underlying structure. It calls us to transcend the illusion of separation, to perceive the unity of all things, to see the divine in the mirror of the mind. It challenges us to awaken to our true nature as conscious beings, co-creators of reality, and active participants in the ongoing creation of the universe.

As we continue our exploration into the heart of quantum spirituality, let this awareness guide us in the dance of life. Let us perceive the world as a reflection of the divine, as a manifestation of consciousness, as a sacred dance of creation. Let us recognize the power of consciousness to shape reality and use that power to create a world that embodies the highest ideals of love, compassion, and unity.

The quantum mind upends the traditional materialistic perspective of reality, inviting us to see consciousness as the bedrock of existence, the source from which all reality springs. This understanding bears profound spiritual implications, urging us to awaken to our true nature as conscious beings, co-creators of reality, and participants in the ongoing creation of the cosmos. As we delve deeper into quantum spirituality, we are invited to transcend the illusion of separation, to perceive the unity of all things, and to witness the divine in the mirror of the mind.

CHAPTER 5: THE QUANTUM LEAP: FROM MIND TO MATTER

In the silent stillness of the cosmos, where the boundaries between thought and reality blur, there lies a profound truth—one that bridges the chasm between the unseen world of the mind and the tangible realm of matter. This truth is the quantum leap, the miraculous process by which consciousness shapes the physical world. It is a journey from the subtle vibrations of thought to the dense manifestations of matter, a transformation that echoes through the very fabric of existence. In this chapter, we explore how the mind influences the physical world, drawing upon the insights of quantum theories of consciousness to reveal how this understanding can lead to healing and transformation on a spiritual level.

The Power of the Quantum Mind

To comprehend the quantum leap from mind to matter, we must first recognize the inherent power of the mind. In the quantum view, the mind is not merely a passive observer of reality but an active participant in the creation of the world. Thoughts, intentions, and beliefs are not ephemeral, insignificant aspects of our existence; they are potent forces that interact with the quantum field, shaping the reality we experience.

Quantum theory teaches us that particles exist in a state of potentiality, a realm of infinite possibilities, until they are observed. It is the act of observation—the focus of consciousness—that collapses the wave function, transforming potential into reality, possibility into certainty. This process is not limited to the microscopic world of particles; it is a universal principle that applies to all aspects of life. The mind, with its focused intentions and beliefs, acts as the observer in the grand quantum experiment of existence, shaping the world in which we live.

The implications of this understanding are profound. If the mind can influence the behaviour of particles, if consciousness can shape reality at the most fundamental level, then our thoughts and intentions have the power to manifest in the physical world. This is the essence of the quantum leap—the sudden, transformative shift from the realm of thought to the realm of matter, from the invisible to the visible, from the potential to the actual.

The Healing Power of Consciousness

One of the most significant applications of the quantum

leap from mind to matter is in the realm of healing. For centuries, traditional medicine has focused on the physical aspects of health, treating the body as a machine that can be repaired through mechanical means. But as our understanding of the mind's influence on matter deepens, we begin to recognize the profound role that consciousness plays in health and healing.

In the quantum view, the body is not a separate, isolated entity but a dynamic, interconnected system, constantly interacting with the mind and the environment. The mind, with its thoughts, emotions, and beliefs, exerts a powerful influence on the body's physiology, shaping the health and well-being of the individual. This understanding forms the basis of what is known as "quantum healing," a process by which the mind influences the body to promote healing and transformation.

Quantum healing is not merely a metaphorical concept; it is supported by a growing body of scientific evidence. Studies have shown that the mind can influence the body's immune system, alter the expression of genes, and even affect the structure of cells. The placebo effect, long considered a curiosity in medical research, is now understood as a powerful demonstration of the mind's ability to influence the body. When a patient believes that they are receiving a treatment, their mind creates physiological changes in the body that mimic the effects of the actual treatment. This is the quantum leap in action—the mind transforming belief into biological reality.

But quantum healing goes beyond the placebo effect. It involves harnessing the power of consciousness to promote healing at the deepest levels of the body and mind. This process begins with the recognition that the mind and body are not separate entities but are interconnected aspects of a unified whole. Thoughts, emotions, and beliefs are not confined to the mind; they are expressed in the body, shaping our health and well-being.

To initiate quantum healing, we must first become aware of the thoughts and beliefs that influence our health. Negative thoughts, fear, anger, and stress create disharmony in the body, disrupting the flow of energy and leading to illness. Conversely, positive thoughts, love, compassion, and peace promote harmony, restoring the natural balance of the body and mind.

The process of quantum healing involves shifting our consciousness from negative, limiting beliefs to positive, empowering ones. This shift is the quantum leap—a sudden, transformative change in consciousness that leads to healing and transformation. By aligning our thoughts and beliefs with the highest ideals of health and well-being, we can influence the quantum field of the body, promoting healing at the cellular and energetic levels.

The Role of Intention in Manifestation

Central to the concept of the quantum leap is the role of intention in manifesting reality. Intention is the focused direction of consciousness, the mental energy that shapes the quantum field and brings potential into actuality. In the process of quantum healing, intention acts as the guiding force, directing the energy of consciousness towards the desired outcome.

Intention is not merely a wish or a hope; it is a powerful force that aligns the mind with the quantum field, creating a resonance that influences the physical world. When we set a clear, focused intention, we send out a wave of energy into the quantum field, collapsing the wave function and manifesting the desired outcome in the physical world.

This process is not limited to healing; it applies to all aspects of life. Whether we seek to manifest health, abundance, love, or success, the principles of the quantum leap remain the same. By focusing our intention and aligning our consciousness with the desired outcome, we can influence the quantum field to bring our desires into reality.

The power of intention is supported by scientific studies that demonstrate the mind's ability to influence the physical world. In experiments on the effects of intention on water, for example, researchers have found that the focused intention of participants can change the molecular structure of water, creating beautiful, harmonious patterns. These experiments demonstrate the power of consciousness to shape the physical world, offering a glimpse into the potential of the quantum leap.

The Spiritual Dimension of Quantum Healing

While the quantum leap from mind to matter has profound implications for physical healing, it also has a deeper, spiritual dimension. At its core, quantum healing is not just about curing the body; it is about transforming the mind and spirit, awakening to our true nature as conscious beings, and aligning our lives with the higher purpose of the soul.

In the process of quantum healing, we begin to recognize that illness is not merely a physical ailment but a manifestation of disharmony in the mind and spirit. The body reflects the state of the mind and spirit, expressing the unresolved conflicts, fears, and traumas that lie hidden within the subconscious. Healing, therefore, requires more than just treating the symptoms of illness; it requires addressing the underlying causes, bringing the mind and spirit into harmony with the body.

This process involves a journey of self-discovery, a deep exploration of the inner world of thoughts, emotions, and beliefs. It requires us to confront the shadows within ourselves, to heal the wounds of the past, and to release the limiting beliefs that hold us back from realizing our full potential. This is the spiritual dimension of quantum healing—a journey of transformation that leads to the awakening of the soul.

As we embark on this journey, we begin to realize that healing is not just about curing the body; it is about awakening to our true nature, aligning our lives with the divine consciousness that pervades the universe, and fulfilling our soul's purpose. This is the ultimate quantum leap—a shift in consciousness that transcends the physical world and connects us with the infinite potential of the soul.

The Practice of Quantum Healing

To engage in quantum healing, we must cultivate a deep awareness of the mind-body connection and develop practices that align our consciousness with the quantum field. These practices include meditation, visualization, affirmation, and mindfulness, all of which help to focus the mind, direct intention, and bring the body into harmony with the mind and spirit.

Meditation is a powerful tool for quantum healing, as it allows us to quiet the mind, enter a state of deep relaxation, and connect with the quantum field of consciousness. In meditation, we can set our intentions, visualize the desired outcome, and align our thoughts and beliefs with the highest ideals of health and well-being.

Visualization is another key practice in quantum healing, as it helps to create a mental image of the desired outcome, bringing the potential into reality. By visualizing health, healing, and harmony, we send out a wave of energy into the quantum field, influencing the body and mind to manifest the desired outcome.

Affirmation is a practice that involves repeating positive statements that reflect the desired outcome. By affirming health, healing, and well-being, we reinforce the positive beliefs that support the process of quantum healing, aligning our consciousness with the quantum field.

Mindfulness is the practice of being fully present in the moment, aware of our thoughts, emotions, and sensations. In the context of quantum healing, mindfulness helps us to become aware of the mind-body connection, recognize the thoughts and beliefs that influence our health, and make conscious choices that support healing and transformation.

These practices are not just techniques; they are ways of

being, ways of aligning our lives with the quantum field of consciousness, and ways of living in harmony with the divine. They are the tools that help us to make the quantum leap from mind to matter, to transform our lives through the power of consciousness.

The Journey of Transformation

As we conclude this chapter, we stand at the threshold of a new understanding of the relationship between mind and matter, a new awareness of the power of consciousness to shape reality. The quantum leap from mind to matter is not just a scientific concept; it is a spiritual journey, a path of healing and transformation that leads to the awakening of the soul.

This journey invites us to recognize the power of the mind to influence the physical world, to harness the energy of consciousness to promote healing, and align our lives with the divine consciousness that pervades the universe. It challenges us to take responsibility for the reality we create, to become conscious co-creators of our lives, and to live in harmony with the quantum field.

The quantum leap is not just a sudden, transformative shift in consciousness; it is a way of life, a way of being that recognizes the interconnectedness of mind and matter, the unity of body and spirit, the harmony of the physical and the divine. It is a journey of self-discovery, a path of healing and transformation, a dance with the infinite potential of the soul.

As we continue our journey into the heart of quantum spirituality, let us carry this awareness with us, and let it guide us in the dance of life. Let us recognize the power of consciousness to shape reality and let us use that power to create a world that reflects the highest ideals of health, healing, and spiritual awakening. Let us make the quantum leap from mind to matter, from thought to reality, from potential to manifestation, and let us live in harmony with the divine consciousness that pervades the universe.

The quantum leap from mind to matter challenges our traditional understanding of reality, inviting us to recognize the power of consciousness to shape the physical world. This understanding has profound implications for healing and transformation, offering a path to spiritual awakening and self-discovery. As we explore the deeper truths of quantum spirituality, we are invited to harness the power of consciousness to promote healing, to align our lives with the divine consciousness that pervades the universe, and to make the quantum leap from mind to matter.

CHAPTER 6: THE SACRED EXPANSE OF THE AKASHIC FIELD

In the boundless, unseen realms of existence, where the echoes of ancient wisdom harmonize with the resonances of the cosmos, there lies a sacred expanse—a universal field that cradles the memory of all that was, all that is, and all that will ever be. This is the Akashic Field, an infinite reservoir of knowledge where every event, thought, and experience is eternally inscribed. The Akashic Field transcends mystical speculation; it stands as a profound reality, a bridge uniting science and spirituality, offering profound insights into the nature of consciousness, time, and the universe itself. In this chapter, we voyage into the heart of this sacred expanse, exploring how the Akashic Field can be accessed through both scientific exploration and spiritual practice.

The Universal Archive of Memory

The notion of the Akashic Field has its roots in ancient spiritual traditions, particularly in the Sanskrit term "Akasha," signifying "ether" or "space." In these traditions, Akasha is revered as the primordial essence of the universe, the medium through which all things are interconnected. It is the womb of creation, the space where the dance of existence unfolds. Thus, the Akashic Field is the cosmic memory of the universe, a living archive that chronicles every action, every thought, every intention.

In the modern era, this ancient concept resonates with scientific explorations of the universe's fundamental structure. The idea that the universe operates as an interconnected field finds support in theories of quantum physics and cosmology. Ervin Laszlo, a trailblazer in this field, posits that the Akashic Field is a tangible, physical phenomenon—a universal field of information permeating all existence.

According to Laszlo, this field, which he dubs the "quantum vacuum," is not a void but a subtle energy field that carries the information of everything that transpires in the universe. This information is neither lost nor dispersed but remains encoded within the field, forming a cosmic memory that can be accessed under certain conditions. The Akashic Field, then, is not merely a mystical abstraction but a scientific reality—a universal field that connects all things and preserves the record of all events.

Accessing the Akashic Field Through Science

Scientific inquiry into the Akashic Field begins with a re-examination of the quantum vacuum, a concept that challenges conventional notions of emptiness. In classical physics, a vacuum is perceived as a void, an absence of matter and energy. Yet, in quantum physics, the vacuum is anything but empty; it is a roiling sea of virtual particles, perpetually flickering in and out of existence. This quantum vacuum is the crucible of all that exists, the ground from which particles and forces emerge.

Laszlo's theory suggests that the quantum vacuum is not merely an energy field but a field of information. This information is not confined to any particular location but is dispersed throughout the field, creating a holographic record of every occurrence in the universe. Just as a hologram encapsulates the entire image in every fragment, so too does the Akashic Field encapsulate the totality of cosmic memory in every point.

The implications of this theory are profound. If the Akashic Field is a genuine, physical phenomenon, it might be possible to access this cosmic memory through scientific means. Research in quantum physics, neuroscience, and consciousness studies is beginning to explore how information is stored and retrieved from this universal field. Experiments in quantum entanglement, for example, suggest that information can be transmitted instantaneously across vast distances, lending credence to the idea that the universe is deeply interconnected and that the Akashic Field may be a key to understanding this interconnectedness.

Moreover, the concept of the Akashic Field challenges our

understanding of time and causality. Within the Akashic Field, past, present, and future do not exist as separate entities but coexist in a timeless now. This suggests that the information stored in the field is not constrained by linear time, opening up the possibility of accessing knowledge of future events as well as past ones. Though controversial, this idea invites new avenues of scientific exploration, urging us to rethink our understanding of time and reality.

The Spiritual Path to the Akashic Field

While science offers one path to exploring the Akashic Field, spiritual traditions provide another. For millennia, mystics, seers, and spiritual practitioners have accessed the Akashic Field through meditation, prayer, and other spiritual practices. These practices are designed to transcend the ordinary limitations of the mind and connect with the deeper layers of consciousness where the Akashic records dwell.

In many spiritual traditions, the Akashic records are envisioned as a vast library or archive, chronicling the soul's journey through time. Accessing these records is not merely an intellectual exercise but a deeply spiritual experience, requiring a state of heightened awareness and alignment with the divine. The records are often said to be guarded by spiritual guides or beings who assist seekers in accessing the information most relevant to their spiritual growth and evolution.

The process of accessing the Akashic records typically involves entering a deep meditative or trance state, where the mind becomes quiet and receptive to the subtle energies of the Akashic Field. In this state, seekers may receive visions, impressions, or intuitive insights that offer guidance and understanding. The information received is often symbolic or metaphorical, requiring careful interpretation and reflection to fully comprehend its meaning.

For those who seek to explore the Akashic Field through spiritual practice, it is essential to approach the experience with humility, reverence, and an open heart. The Akashic records are not merely a repository of knowledge; they are a sacred space, a reflection of the divine intelligence permeating the universe. Accessing this space is both a privilege and a responsibility, demanding that seekers align with the highest principles of truth, love, and compassion.

The Healing Potential of the Akashic Field

One of the most profound aspects of the Akashic Field is its potential for healing and transformation. The records stored within the Akashic Field are not static; they are dynamic and responsive to the consciousness of the individual. By accessing these records, one can gain insight into the root causes of physical, emotional, and spiritual challenges, facilitating healing at the deepest levels of the soul.

Healing through the Akashic Field involves identifying and releasing patterns of thought, emotion, and behaviour that contribute to imbalance or disharmony. These patterns are often rooted in past experiences, whether in this lifetime or in previous ones, and are stored within the Akashic records as energetic imprints. By bringing these patterns into awareness, it is possible to transform them, releasing the energy trapped in limiting beliefs and emotions, and restoring the natural flow of life force energy.

This healing process is not merely about addressing specific issues but about awakening to the deeper truth of who we are. The Akashic Field holds the memory of the soul's journey, the lessons learned, the challenges overcome, and the growth achieved. By accessing this sacred space, we can gain a broader perspective on our lives, understanding the purpose behind our experiences and the opportunities for growth and transformation they present.

The healing power of the Akashic Field extends beyond the individual to the collective. As we heal ourselves, we contribute to the healing of the collective consciousness, releasing the patterns of fear, separation, and conflict that have shaped human history. The Akashic Field, with its record of all that has been, offers us the opportunity to rewrite the narrative of humanity, creating a new story rooted in love, unity, and peace.

The Akashic Field and the Evolution of Consciousness

The concept of the Akashic Field also carries profound implications for the evolution of consciousness. As we deepen our connection with this universal field, we open ourselves to new levels of awareness, expanding our understanding of the nature of reality and our place within it. The Akashic Field serves as a bridge between the individual and the collective, the personal and the universal, the finite and the infinite.

In the process of spiritual evolution, the Akashic Field acts as a guide, offering insights and wisdom that support our growth and development. As we align with the higher frequencies of the Akashic Field, we begin to resonate with the consciousness of the cosmos, attuning ourselves to the divine intelligence that shapes the universe. This alignment brings about a shift in perspective, enabling us to perceive the interconnectedness of all life and to recognize our role as co-creators of reality.

The evolution of consciousness is not merely an individual journey; it is a collective process, a movement toward greater unity, harmony, and understanding. The Akashic Field, with its record of the soul's journey, provides an opportunity to learn from the past, heal the wounds of history, and create a future that reflects the highest ideals of humanity. It invites us to participate in the unfolding of the cosmic plan, to contribute to the evolution of consciousness, and to fulfil our highest potential as spiritual beings.

The Sacred Science of the Akashic Field

As we explore the Akashic Field, we find ourselves at the confluence of science and spirituality, where the boundaries between the two begin to dissolve. The Akashic Field is not merely a mystical concept or a scientific hypothesis; it is a sacred science, a way of understanding the universe that integrates the wisdom of both disciplines.

In this sacred science, we recognize that the universe is not a collection of isolated, independent entities but a vast, interconnected web of energy and information. The Akashic Field is the medium through which this interconnectedness is expressed, the space where the dance of creation unfolds. It is the bridge between the seen and the unseen, the physical and the spiritual, the temporal and the eternal.

The sacred science of the Akashic Field challenges us to transcend the dualities that have shaped our understanding of reality and to embrace a more holistic, integrative view of existence. It urges

us to see the universe not as a mechanical system governed by impersonal laws but as a living, conscious entity imbued with divine intelligence and purpose. It calls us to explore the deeper dimensions of existence, to access the wisdom of the Akashic Field, and to use that wisdom to create a world that reflects the highest ideals of love, compassion, and unity.

The Journey Into the Akashic Field

As we conclude this chapter, we stand at the threshold of a profound understanding of the universe, a new awareness of the sacred expanse that is the Akashic Field. This field, with its record of all that has been, all that is, and all that will ever be, offers us the opportunity to explore the deeper dimensions of existence, to gain insight into the nature of consciousness, and to participate in the unfolding of the cosmic plan.

The journey into the Akashic Field is not merely a scientific exploration or a spiritual practice; it is a sacred journey, a path of awakening that leads us to the heart of the universe. It invites us to explore the memory of the cosmos, to access the wisdom of the Akashic records, and to use that wisdom to create a world that embodies the highest ideals of humanity.

As we continue our exploration into the heart of quantum spirituality, let us carry this awareness with us, allowing it to guide us in the dance of life. Let us recognize the sacred expanse of the Akashic Field, the universal archive of memory that connects all things, and let us use that connection to heal, transform, and awaken to the truth of our existence.

The Akashic Field offers a profound understanding of the universe as a vast, interconnected web of energy and information. By accessing this sacred space, we can gain insights into the nature of consciousness, heal the wounds of the past, and contribute to the evolution of humanity. As we delve into the deeper truths of quantum spirituality, we are invited to recognize the Akashic Field as a bridge between science and spirituality, a sacred expanse that connects all things, and a source of wisdom and guidance for our journey into the heart of the cosmos.

CHAPTER 7: THE ENIGMATIC QUANTUM CONSCIOUSNESS

In the dimly lit corridors of quantum theory, where the familiar laws of physics begin to waver like a mirage, lies an enigma that has perplexed scientists and philosophers alike—a puzzle that touches the very core of existence. This enigma is the mysterious relationship between quantum mechanics and consciousness, a relationship that suggests our thoughts and observations are not mere passive reflections of reality but active participants in its creation. As we delve into this profound mystery, we are invited to contemplate the implications for our understanding of the universe and our place within it—a contemplation that inevitably leads us to the threshold of spirituality.

The Quantum Enigma: The Observer and the Observed

The quantum world, at first glance, appears to be a domain governed by strange and counterintuitive principles—particles that exist in multiple states simultaneously, waves that behave like particles, and probabilities that only become realities upon observation. One of the most perplexing aspects of quantum mechanics is the role of the observer, a role that challenges our conventional understanding of reality.

In classical physics, the world is seen as an objective reality, independent of the observer. Objects exist in a definite state, whether or not they are being observed. However, quantum mechanics turns this notion on its head. In the quantum realm, particles such as electrons and photons do not have definite properties until they are measured or observed. Until that moment, they exist in a state of superposition—a blend of all possible states. It is the act of observation that collapses this superposition into a single, definite outcome.

This phenomenon is encapsulated in the famous double-slit experiment, where particles passing through two slits create an interference pattern indicative of wave behaviour when not observed. However, when observed, the particles behave like discrete particles, creating two distinct bands on the detection screen. The very act of observation changes the outcome—a mystery that lies at the heart of quantum mechanics.

This "observer effect" suggests that consciousness plays a crucial role in the manifestation of reality. It implies that reality is not a fixed, objective entity but is instead influenced, and perhaps even created, by the consciousness that observes it. This idea challenges the traditional materialistic view of the universe and invites us to explore the deeper relationship between consciousness and the physical world.

The Mind as a Co-Creator of Reality

The implications of the observer effect are profound. If consciousness plays a role in shaping reality, then the mind is not just a passive observer of the world but an active participant in its creation. This understanding opens the door to a new paradigm, where the mind is seen as a co-creator of reality, working in concert with the quantum field to bring forth the world we experience.

This perspective aligns with ancient spiritual teachings, which have long suggested that the mind has the power to shape reality. The idea that "thoughts are things" is not just a metaphor but a reflection of a deeper truth. In the quantum view, the mind interacts with the quantum field, collapsing the wave function and bringing potentialities into actuality. The thoughts and intentions we hold in our minds influence the fabric of reality, shaping the world in ways that are both subtle and profound.

This understanding challenges us to reconsider the nature of reality and the role of consciousness within it. It suggests that reality is not a fixed, immutable structure but a dynamic, fluid process, constantly being shaped and reshaped by the consciousness that perceives it. The world we experience is not separate from us; it reflects our own consciousness, a mirror that reflects the thoughts, beliefs, and intentions we hold within our minds.

The Quantum Mind: A Bridge Between Science and Spirituality

The mysterious relationship between quantum mechanics and consciousness offers a bridge between science and spirituality—a bridge that invites us to explore the deeper dimensions of reality and to recognize the unity of mind and matter. In the quantum view, the mind is not confined to the brain; it is a field of consciousness that interacts with the quantum field, influencing the behaviour of particles and shaping the world we experience.

This understanding resonates with spiritual teachings that emphasize the interconnectedness of all things and the power of consciousness to create reality. In many spiritual traditions, the mind is seen as a reflection of the divine consciousness that pervades the universe—a consciousness that is both immanent and transcendent, both within and beyond the physical world.

The concept of quantum consciousness suggests that the mind is not just a product of the brain but a fundamental aspect of reality—a bridge between the physical and the spiritual, the finite and the infinite. It invites us to explore the deeper dimensions of our own consciousness, to recognize the divine within ourselves, and to embrace our role as co-creators of reality.

The Mystery of Nonlocality and Entanglement

One of the most intriguing aspects of quantum mechanics is the phenomenon of nonlocality, which suggests that particles can be instantaneously connected, regardless of the distance between them.

This phenomenon, known as quantum entanglement, challenges our traditional understanding of space and time and suggests that the universe is deeply interconnected in ways that transcend physical boundaries.

In the famous thought experiment known as "Schrödinger's cat," a cat is placed in a sealed box with a radioactive atom that has a 50% chance of decaying. If the atom decays, it triggers a mechanism that kills the cat. If it doesn't decay, the cat remains alive. According to quantum mechanics, until the box is opened and the cat is observed, it exists in a superposition of states—both alive and dead. This thought experiment illustrates the strange and counterintuitive nature of quantum mechanics, where the act of observation collapses multiple possibilities into a single reality.

Entanglement takes this mystery even further. When two particles become entangled, the state of one particle instantly influences the state of the other, no matter how far apart they are. This instantaneous connection defies the speed of light and suggests that the universe is not bound by the limitations of space and time. Instead, it operates as a unified whole, where all things are connected in a web of relationships that transcends physical boundaries.

The phenomenon of entanglement offers a glimpse into the deeper reality that lies beneath the surface of the physical world—a reality where consciousness, energy, and information are interconnected in ways that defy our conventional understanding. It suggests that the mind is not separate from the world but is intricately connected to the quantum field, influencing and being influenced by the web of relationships that make up the fabric of reality.

The Spiritual Implications of Quantum Consciousness

The enigmatic relationship between quantum mechanics and consciousness has profound implications for spirituality. It challenges us to reconsider our understanding of the self, the universe, and the nature of reality, inviting us to explore the deeper dimensions of existence and to recognize the unity of mind and matter.

In the quantum view, the self is not a fixed, isolated entity but a dynamic, evolving process, shaped by the interplay of consciousness and the quantum field. The boundaries between self and other, mind and matter, subject and object, begin to dissolve, revealing the interconnectedness of all things.

This understanding invites us to transcend the illusion of separation and to embrace a more holistic, integrative view of reality. It calls us to recognize the divine within ourselves and within the world, to see the universe as a reflection of consciousness, and to participate in the ongoing creation of reality.

The spiritual implications of quantum consciousness extend beyond the individual to the collective. As we awaken to the deeper dimensions of consciousness, we contribute to the evolution of collective consciousness, helping to create a world that reflects the highest ideals of love, compassion, and unity. The quantum leap from mind to matter is not just a personal journey; it is a collective transformation, a movement towards greater awareness, harmony, and understanding.

The Challenge of the Quantum Enigma

The quantum enigma challenges us to confront the mystery of existence, to explore the deeper dimensions of reality, and to embrace the profound implications for our understanding of the self, the universe, and the nature of consciousness. It invites us to move beyond the limitations of materialism and to explore the spiritual dimensions of existence, recognizing the unity of mind and matter, consciousness and the physical world.

This challenge is not just an intellectual exercise; it is a call to spiritual awakening, a journey into the heart of the mystery that lies at the core of existence. It invites us to explore the deeper dimensions of our own consciousness, to recognize the divine within ourselves and within the world, and to participate in the ongoing creation of reality.

The quantum enigma is not a problem to be solved but a mystery to be embraced—a mystery that invites us to explore the deeper dimensions of reality and to recognize the unity of mind and matter, consciousness and the physical world. It is a call to awaken to the deeper truth of who we are, to embrace our role as co-creators of reality, and to participate in the ongoing evolution of consciousness.

The Journey Into Quantum Consciousness

As we conclude this chapter, we find ourselves standing at the threshold of a new understanding of the universe, a new awareness of the enigmatic relationship between quantum mechanics and consciousness. This relationship challenges our conventional understanding of reality and invites us to explore the deeper dimensions of existence, recognizing the unity of mind and matter, consciousness and the physical world.

The journey into quantum consciousness is not just a scientific inquiry or a philosophical exploration; it is a spiritual journey, a path of awakening that leads us to the heart of the mystery that lies at the core of existence. It invites us to recognize the divine within ourselves and within the world, to embrace our role as co-creators of reality, and to participate in the ongoing evolution of consciousness.

As we continue our journey into the heart of quantum spirituality, let us carry this awareness with us, and let it guide us in the dance of life. Let us embrace the mystery of the quantum enigma, recognizing the unity of mind and matter, consciousness and the physical world, and let us use that awareness to create a world that reflects the highest ideals of love, compassion, and unity.

The enigmatic relationship between quantum mechanics and consciousness challenges our conventional understanding of reality and invites us to explore the deeper dimensions of existence. This exploration has profound implications for spirituality, calling us to recognize the unity of mind and matter, consciousness and the physical world, and to embrace our role as co-creators of reality. As we delve into the mystery of quantum consciousness, we are invited to awaken to the deeper truth of who we are and to participate in the ongoing evolution of consciousness.

CHAPTER 8: THE INFINITE EXPANSE OF POSSIBILITY

In the limitless tapestry of the cosmos, where the known and unknown interlace in an eternal symphony, there exists a profound and enigmatic realm—a field of infinite possibilities. This quantum field, a cornerstone of modern physics, transcends mere scientific abstraction; it is the very essence of reality, where all potentialities coexist, awaiting the touch of consciousness to bring them into being. In this chapter, we journey into the heart of this quantum field, uncovering how understanding its nature can empower us to shape both our spiritual and physical realities, unlocking the boundless potential within us.

The Quantum Field: A Realm Beyond Time and Space

At the heart of quantum physics lies a radical understanding: the universe is not a collection of isolated objects but a vast, interconnected field of energy and information. This field, often termed the quantum field, is the foundational matrix of reality—a realm where all possibilities exist simultaneously, unbound by the constraints of time and space.

In classical physics, reality is perceived as a linear sequence of cause and effect, with objects occupying definite states at specific moments. However, the quantum field defies this linearity. It is a domain of superposition, where particles can exist in multiple states simultaneously, and where the future is not a predetermined path but a complex web of potential outcomes, each as real as the next until observed.

This concept of the quantum field as a realm of infinite possibilities is both exhilarating and humbling. It reveals a universe that is far more fluid and dynamic than we have been taught to believe—one in which reality is not a fixed, immutable structure but a living, breathing process, continually shaped and reshaped by the consciousness that interacts with it.

The Power of Potential: Embracing Superposition

One of the most intriguing aspects of the quantum field is the concept of superposition, which posits that particles exist in a state of potential until they are observed. In this state, a particle is not confined to a single location or state; it exists in all possible locations and states simultaneously. Superposition is a fundamental characteristic of the quantum world, reflecting the infinite possibilities that lie within the quantum field.

Consider Schrödinger's famous thought experiment, where a cat is placed in a sealed box with a radioactive atom that has a 50% chance of decaying. If the atom decays, the cat is poisoned and dies; if the atom does not decay, the cat lives. According to quantum mechanics, until the box is opened and observed, the cat exists in a superposition of states—both alive and dead. This paradox highlights the strange, counterintuitive nature of the quantum field, where all possibilities coexist until a conscious observation collapses them into a single reality.

The concept of superposition invites us to reconsider our relationship with reality. It suggests that the world we experience is not predetermined or fixed but is instead a fluid, malleable process shaped by our consciousness. The possibilities within the quantum field are not confined by the constraints of physical reality; they are limitless, awaiting the focus of our minds to bring them into existence.

The Observer Effect: Consciousness Shapes Reality

Central to the quantum field is the observer effect—the principle that the act of observation collapses the superposition of possibilities into a singular, definite outcome. This effect implies that consciousness is a crucial element in the creation of reality, suggesting that the world we experience is profoundly influenced by the thoughts, beliefs, and intentions we hold.

The observer effect challenges the traditional notion of an objective reality that exists independently of our perception. Instead, it posits that reality is a co-creation between the observer and the observed, between consciousness and the quantum field. The world is not something that merely happens to us; it is something we actively participate in creating.

This understanding of the observer effect empowers us to take responsibility for the reality we experience. It encourages us to recognize the immense power of our thoughts and intentions in shaping the world around us. By directing our consciousness towards the possibilities, we wish to manifest, we can collapse the infinite potential of the quantum field into a reality that reflects our highest aspirations.

Creating Our Reality: The Power of Intention

If the quantum field is a realm of infinite possibilities, and if consciousness plays a role in shaping reality, then our intentions are powerful tools for creation. Intention is the focused direction of consciousness, the mental force that interacts with the quantum field to bring potentialities into being. By setting clear, focused intentions, we can influence the quantum field and shape our spiritual and physical realities.

The power of intention is not merely a philosophical idea; it is supported by scientific research demonstrating the mind's ability to influence the physical world. Experiments in quantum physics, such as the double-slit experiment, show that the simple act of observation can alter the behaviour of particles. Similarly, studies in consciousness research reveal that focused intention can affect everything from the growth of plants to the healing of the body.

To harness the power of intention, it is essential to cultivate a deep awareness of our thoughts and beliefs. The quantum field responds not only to our conscious intentions but also to the underlying beliefs and emotions that shape our consciousness. Negative thoughts, limiting beliefs, and unresolved emotions can create interference patterns in the quantum field, hindering the manifestation of our desired outcomes.

The practice of setting intentions involves aligning our thoughts, beliefs, and emotions with the possibilities we wish to bring into reality. This process begins with clarity —identifying what we truly desire and focusing our consciousness on that outcome. It also requires releasing limiting beliefs or negative emotions that may obstruct our intentions. By aligning our consciousness with the infinite possibilities of the quantum field, we can bring our intentions into reality.

The Role of Visualization in Manifestation

Visualization is a potent tool for interacting with the quantum field and manifesting our intentions. By creating a vivid mental image of the desired outcome, we project a wave of energy into the quantum field, influencing the superposition of possibilities and collapsing them into a singular, definite reality.

Visualization involves more than merely seeing the desired outcome in the mind's eye; it also involves experiencing the emotions associated with that outcome. Emotions are a powerful form of energy, playing a crucial role in shaping the quantum field. When we visualize an outcome imbued with positive emotions—such as joy, love, and gratitude—we create a resonance between our consciousness and the quantum field, amplifying the power of our intentions.

Visualization is not just a mental exercise; it is an active engagement with the quantum field, a method of bringing the infinite possibilities of the quantum realm into the physical world. By practicing visualization, we can become conscious creators of our reality, moulding the world according to our highest aspirations.

The Spiritual Dimension of the Quantum Field

The quantum field is not merely a physical phenomenon; it is also a spiritual reality, a manifestation of the divine intelligence that permeates the universe. In many spiritual traditions, the concept of the quantum field resonates with the notion of the divine matrix—a space in which all things are interconnected, where all possibilities exist, and where the divine interacts with creation.

From this perspective, the quantum field is not just an expanse of energy and information; it is a sacred space, an expression of the divine consciousness that creates and sustains the universe. The infinite possibilities within the quantum field are reflections of divine will, opportunities for the soul to evolve, grow, and fulfil its purpose.

The spiritual dimension of the quantum field invites us to acknowledge our connection to the divine, to see ourselves as co-creators with the divine intelligence that shapes the cosmos. It challenges us to align our intentions with the highest principles of love, compassion, and unity, and to use the power of the quantum field to create a world that embodies these principles.

By embracing the spiritual dimension of the quantum field, we can transform our relationship with reality. We can shift from a mindset of limitation and scarcity to one of abundance and possibility. We can recognize that the universe is a supportive, responsive environment, eager to assist us in realizing our highest potential.

The Journey of Creation

The field of infinite possibilities offers us a profound insight into the nature of reality—a reality that is fluid, dynamic, and responsive to our consciousness. It beckons us to become conscious creators of our lives, to recognize the power we possess to shape our spiritual and physical realities, and to embrace the limitless potential within us.

This journey of creation is not merely about manifesting our desires; it is about aligning our lives with the divine intelligence that infuses the universe. It is about recognizing the interconnectedness of all things, the unity of mind and matter, and the sacredness of the quantum field. It is about using the power of intention, visualization, and spiritual practice to create a reality that reflects our highest aspirations and values.

As we continue our exploration into the heart of quantum spirituality, let us carry this awareness with us, allowing it to guide us in the dance of life. Let us recognize the field of infinite possibilities as a sacred space, a realm where all potential realities exist, waiting to be brought into being by the touch of consciousness. Let us embrace our role as co-creators with the divine and use that role to create a world that reflects the highest ideals of love, compassion, and unity.

The quantum field, as a realm of infinite possibilities, offers a profound understanding of reality and our role as conscious creators. By understanding the nature of this field and the power of our intentions, we can shape our spiritual and physical realities, unlocking the limitless potential that lies within us. As we delve into the deeper truths of quantum spirituality, we are invited to embrace the field of infinite possibilities as a sacred space, a reflection of the divine intelligence that permeates the universe, and a source of empowerment for creating a life that embodies our highest aspirations.

CHAPTER 9: THE SACRED GEOMETRY OF THE UNIVERSE

In the silent symphony of the cosmos, where stars are born in spirals of fire and galaxies waltz through the void, there lies an underlying order—a divine architecture that weaves together the fabric of existence. This is the sacred geometry of the universe, an ancient and profound truth that speaks of patterns so perfect, so harmonious, that they seem to echo the thoughts of the divine itself. From the spirals of seashells to the orbits of planets, from the dance of subatomic particles to the unfolding of a rose, this geometry is the blueprint of creation, a testament to the unity and wholeness that pervades all things.

In this chapter, we shall delve into the mysteries of sacred geometry, exploring how these patterns underlie both the visible and invisible realms of existence. Drawing inspiration from David Bohm's concept of the "Implicate Order," we will journey into the heart of the universe's design, where the physical and the spiritual intertwine in a dance of exquisite symmetry and beauty.

The Language of Creation: Understanding Sacred Geometry

Sacred geometry is the language of creation, the code by which the universe expresses its infinite complexity in forms that are both simple and profound. It is the study of shapes, patterns, and proportions that are fundamental to the structure of the cosmos, reflecting the underlying unity of all things. From the smallest atom to the largest galaxy, from the molecular bonds in our DNA to the vast networks of the brain, sacred geometry is the blueprint that shapes all of existence.

At the heart of sacred geometry lies the understanding that the universe is not a random, chaotic assembly of matter, but a harmonious, interconnected whole. Every form, every structure, every phenomenon in the universe follows certain geometric principles, which are expressions of deeper, universal laws. These patterns are not just mathematical abstractions; they are the very essence of reality, the means by which the infinite potential of the universe is made manifest in the physical world.

The most well-known example of sacred geometry is the Flower of Life, a symbol that has been found in cultures around the world, from ancient Egypt to modern-day spiritual practices. The Flower of Life is composed of multiple, evenly spaced, overlapping circles arranged in a hexagonal pattern. This simple yet profound pattern is said to contain the blueprint for all of creation, representing the interconnectedness of all life and the fundamental structure of the universe.

Another fundamental shape in sacred geometry is the Golden Ratio, also known as the Divine Proportion. This ratio, approximately 1.618, is a mathematical constant that appears in the proportions of countless natural forms, from the spirals of galaxies to the human body, from the branching of trees to the structure of crystals. The Golden Ratio is a manifestation of the universe's inherent harmony, a reflection of the divine order that pervades all things.

In the quantum realm, these geometric principles take on new and profound meanings. The behaviour of subatomic particles, the structure of energy fields, and the patterns of quantum entanglement all reflect the same underlying geometric order. Just as a crystal is formed from the regular arrangement of atoms, so too is the quantum field structured according to principles of sacred geometry, revealing the unity of all things at the most fundamental level.

The Implicate Order: The Universe as a Unified Whole

David Bohm, a physicist and philosopher, introduced the concept of the Implicate Order, a profound idea that challenges our traditional understanding of the universe. According to Bohm, the universe is not a collection of separate, independent objects, but a unified whole, where all things are interconnected in ways that transcend the limitations of space and time.

In the Implicate Order, every part of the universe contains the whole, just as every part of a hologram contains the entire image. This idea is closely related to the concept of holonomy, the principle that the whole is present in every part. In this view, the universe is a dynamic, flowing process, where all things are enfolded within each other, creating a seamless web of relationships that connect the entire cosmos.

The Implicate Order is the underlying structure of reality, the hidden dimension where the unity of all things is revealed. In this realm, the boundaries between self and other, mind and matter, subject and object begin to dissolve, revealing the interconnectedness of all existence. The physical world, with its apparent separateness and fragmentation, is an expression of the Explicate Order, the unfolded reality that emerges from the deeper, hidden dimensions of the Implicate Order.

Sacred geometry is a manifestation of the Implicate Order, the visible expression of the deeper unity that underlies all things. The patterns and shapes that we see in the physical world are not random or arbitrary; they are reflections of the deeper order that pervades the universe. Just as a seed contains within it the blueprint for the entire plant, so too does the Implicate Order contain the blueprint for the entire cosmos, a blueprint that is expressed through the sacred geometry of the universe.

The Spiral: The Dance of Creation

One of the most fundamental and ubiquitous patterns in sacred geometry is the spiral. The spiral is a symbol of growth, evolution, and transformation, a pattern that can be found in everything from the shells of snails to the structure of galaxies, from the arrangement of seeds in a sunflower to the DNA in our cells. The spiral is a manifestation of the dynamic, ever-unfolding nature of the universe, a reflection of the continuous process of creation and evolution.

In sacred geometry, the spiral is often associated with the Fibonacci sequence, a series of numbers where each number is the sum of the two preceding ones. This sequence, which begins with 0, 1, 1, 2, 3, 5, 8, 13, and so on, generates a spiral pattern that is found throughout nature. The Fibonacci spiral is a manifestation of the Golden Ratio, and it reflects the inherent harmony and balance that pervades the universe.

The spiral is also a symbol of the journey of the soul, the path of spiritual evolution and transformation. Just as the spiral expands outward from a central point, so too does the soul evolve and grow, moving from the centre of its being into the infinite possibilities of existence. The spiral is a reminder that life is a continuous process of growth and transformation, a journey that takes us ever closer to the divine.

In the quantum realm, the spiral takes on new and profound meanings. The behaviour of particles, the structure of energy fields, and the patterns of quantum entanglement all reflect the spiral's underlying order. The spiral is a symbol of the unity of all things, a reflection of the divine order that pervades the universe.

The Mandala: The Circle of Wholeness

Another fundamental symbol in sacred geometry is the mandala, a geometric design that represents the universe in its entirety. The mandala is typically composed of a circle, with various shapes and patterns radiating from the centre. The circle is a symbol of unity, wholeness, and infinity, a reflection of the divine order that pervades the universe.

In many spiritual traditions, the mandala is used as a tool for meditation and contemplation, a means of connecting with the deeper dimensions of the self and the universe. The mandala reflects the soul's journey, a map of the inner landscape that guides us towards wholeness and integration.

The mandala is also a symbol of the cosmic order, the underlying structure that shapes the universe. The patterns and shapes that we see in the mandala are not random or arbitrary; they are reflections of the deeper order that pervades the universe. Just as the circle is a symbol of unity, so too is the mandala a reflection of the unity of all things.

In the quantum realm, the mandala takes on new and profound meanings. The behaviour of particles, the structure of energy fields, and the patterns of quantum entanglement all reflect the mandala's underlying order. The mandala is a symbol of the unity of all things, a reflection of the divine order that pervades the universe.

The Cube: The Structure of Reality

The cube is another fundamental shape in sacred geometry, representing the structure and stability of the physical world. The cube is composed of six faces, twelve edges, and eight vertices, and it is associated with the element of earth. The cube is a symbol of the material world, the foundation upon which all things are built.

In sacred geometry, the cube is often associated with the

Platonic solid known as the hexahedron. The hexahedron is one of the five Platonic solids, which are the only regular polyhedra that exist in three dimensions. These solids are considered to be the building blocks of the universe, the fundamental shapes that underlie all of reality.

The cube is also a symbol of balance and harmony, representing the equilibrium that exists in the universe. Just as the cube is a stable, balanced shape, so too is the universe a stable, balanced system, where all things are interconnected and in harmony.

In the quantum realm, the cube takes on new and profound meanings. The behaviour of particles, the structure of energy fields, and the patterns of quantum entanglement all reflect the cube's underlying order. The cube is a symbol of the unity of all things, a reflection of the divine order that pervades the universe.

The Interconnectedness of All Things

Sacred geometry reflects the interconnectedness of all things, a testament to the unity and wholeness that pervades the universe. The patterns and shapes that we see in the physical world are not random or arbitrary; they are expressions of the deeper order that underlies all of reality. This order is the manifestation of the divine intelligence that pervades the universe, the blueprint for all of creation.

The interconnectedness of all things is a fundamental principle of quantum physics, where the behaviour of particles is influenced by their relationships with other particles, regardless of distance. This phenomenon, known as quantum entanglement, reflects the deeper unity that underlies all of existence. In the quantum realm, there are no separate, independent objects; everything is interconnected, woven together in a seamless web of relationships that transcends the limitations of space and time.

This interconnectedness is also reflected in the spiritual traditions of the world, which teach that all things are one, that the self is not separate from the world, but is part of the greater whole. The patterns of sacred geometry are a reminder of this unity, a reflection of the divine order that pervades the universe.

The Dance of Creation: The Universe as a Living Being

Sacred geometry is not just a static, unchanging structure; it is a dynamic, living process, a dance of creation that is constantly unfolding. The universe is not a fixed, immutable entity, but a living, breathing being, constantly evolving and growing. The patterns of sacred geometry are the expressions of this dynamic process, the visible manifestations of the divine intelligence that shapes the cosmos.

In the quantum realm, the dance of creation takes on new and profound meanings. The behaviour of particles, the structure of energy fields, and the patterns of quantum entanglement all reflect the dynamic, ever-changing nature of the universe. The universe is not a static, unchanging entity, but a living, breathing process, constantly evolving and growing.

This understanding challenges us to see the universe not as a collection of separate, independent objects, but as a unified whole, where all things are interconnected and in harmony. It invites us to recognize the divine intelligence that pervades the universe, and to see the patterns of sacred geometry as the expressions of this intelligence.

The Journey into the Sacred Geometry of the Universe

As we conclude this chapter, we find ourselves standing at the threshold of a new understanding of the universe, a new awareness of the sacred geometry that underlies all of reality. This geometry is not just a mathematical abstraction; it is the very essence of existence, the blueprint for all of creation. It reflects the divine intelligence that pervades the universe, how the infinite potential of the cosmos is made manifest in the physical world.

The journey into the sacred geometry of the universe is not just a scientific inquiry or a philosophical exploration; it is a spiritual journey, a path of awakening that leads us to the heart of the divine. It invites us to recognize the interconnectedness of all things, to see the universe as a unified whole, and to embrace the patterns of sacred geometry as the expressions of the divine order that pervades the cosmos.

As we continue our journey into the heart of quantum spirituality, let us carry this awareness with us, and let it guide us in the dance of life. Let us recognize the sacred geometry of the universe as a reflection of the divine intelligence that shapes all of creation and let us use that recognition to create a world that reflects the highest ideals of love, compassion, and unity.

The sacred geometry of the universe offers a profound

understanding of the patterns and structures that underlie all of reality. By recognizing these patterns as expressions of the divine intelligence that pervades the cosmos, we can deepen our understanding of the interconnectedness of all things and our place within the greater whole. As we explore the deeper truths of quantum spirituality, we are invited to embrace the sacred geometry of the universe as a reflection of the divine order, a testament to the unity and wholeness that pervades all of existence.

CHAPTER 10: THE QUANTUM HEART: WEAVING THE THREADS OF SCIENCE AND SPIRITUALITY

In the silent, rhythmic cadence of the heart lies a profound enigma—a mystery that beats in harmony with the pulse of the cosmos and bridges the worlds of science and spirituality. Often regarded merely as the organ that sustains life, the heart is, in truth, a vessel of far deeper significance. It is the seat of consciousness, a fountain of emotion, and the nexus where the quantum world meets the spiritual realm. In this chapter, we delve into the quantum heart, exploring how its powerful electromagnetic field influences reality and how we can harness this extraordinary force for spiritual growth and transformation.

The Heart as the Centre of Being

For millennia, the heart has been venerated as the centre of human experience. Ancient civilizations revered the heart as the seat of the soul, the wellspring of wisdom, and the core of our emotional and spiritual lives. In many spiritual traditions, the heart is seen not merely as a physical organ but as a gateway to higher consciousness, a bridge between the material and the divine.

Modern science, too, is beginning to recognize the extraordinary nature of the heart. Research in fields such as neurocardiology has revealed that the heart possesses its own intricate nervous system, often called the "heart-brain." This heart-brain is capable of processing information, making decisions, and even exerting influence over the brain in profound ways. The heart is not simply a passive pump; it is an active participant in our emotional, cognitive, and spiritual processes.

But the heart's influence reaches far beyond its physiological role. The heart generates the most potent electromagnetic field in the human body, one that is over 5,000 times stronger than the field produced by the brain. This electromagnetic field extends beyond the confines of the physical body, radiating outward and interacting with the quantum field that underpins all of reality.

The Electromagnetic Symphony of the Heart

The heart's electromagnetic field is a dynamic, living force that interacts with the quantum field, influencing the world around us in subtle yet profound ways. This field is not merely a byproduct of the heart's physical activity; it is a manifestation of the heart's deeper, spiritual essence—a reflection of the energies of love, compassion, and consciousness.

The electromagnetic field generated by the heart forms a torus-shaped structure, often depicted as a continuous loop of energy flowing outward from the heart, encircling the body, and then returning to the heart. This toroidal field is a fundamental pattern found throughout nature, symbolizing wholeness and the interconnectedness of all things. It is a shape that can be seen in everything from the structure of galaxies to the dynamics of subatomic particles, a testament to the underlying unity of the universe.

This toroidal field is not static or unchanging; it is a dynamic, living process, constantly interacting with the quantum field and the fields of other beings. The heart's electromagnetic field serves as a bridge between the physical and the spiritual, a conduit through which our thoughts, emotions, and intentions can influence the quantum field, shaping the reality we experience.

The Heart and the Quantum Field

The heart's electromagnetic field is a powerful tool for engaging with the quantum field—the foundational fabric of reality where all possibilities exist. In the quantum field, particles do not possess definite properties until observed; they remain in a state of potential, awaiting the focus of consciousness to bring them into reality. The heart, with its potent electromagnetic field, plays a pivotal role in this process of manifestation.

The heart's electromagnetic field is deeply intertwined with our emotional states, which in turn influence our thoughts and intentions. Positive emotions such as love, gratitude, and compassion generate a coherent, harmonious electromagnetic field, which interacts with the quantum field in ways that promote health, well-being, and the realization of our highest aspirations. Conversely, negative emotions like fear, anger, and resentment create a chaotic, disordered field, disrupting the quantum field and leading to experiences of disharmony and dis-ease.

This understanding of the heart's electromagnetic field invites us to cultivate awareness of our emotional states and to foster emotions that promote coherence and harmony. By aligning our emotions with the higher frequencies of love and compassion, we can influence the quantum field in ways that support our spiritual growth and the fulfilment of our true potential.

The Heart as a Portal to Higher Consciousness

The heart is not only a bridge between the physical and quantum realms; it is also a portal to higher consciousness, a gateway through which we can access deeper levels of awareness and connect with the divine. Many spiritual traditions speak of the heart as the "seat of the soul," the meeting place of the human and the divine, where the individual self merges with the universal self.

Awakening the heart involves shifting our focus from the mind to the heart, from the intellectual to the intuitive, from the ego to the soul. This shift is not merely a change in perspective; it is a transformation of consciousness, a movement from separation to unity, from fear to love, from limitation to infinity.

When the heart is fully awakened, it becomes a powerful instrument for spiritual growth and transformation. It allows us to access deeper levels of intuition and wisdom, connect with the higher aspects of our being, and experience the oneness of all life. The heart's electromagnetic field acts as a channel for this higher consciousness, enabling us to bring the light of the soul into our daily lives and to manifest our highest aspirations in the world.

Heart Coherence: Resonating with the Divine

One of the most potent practices for harnessing the energy of the heart is the practice of heart coherence. Heart coherence is a state of alignment between the heart, mind, and emotions, where the electromagnetic field of the heart becomes coherent and harmonious. This state of coherence is not just a physiological state; it is a spiritual state, a reflection of our alignment with the divine.

When we achieve heart coherence, we align our consciousness with the higher frequencies of love, compassion, and unity. This alignment creates a resonance between our electromagnetic field and the quantum field, amplifying our intentions and enabling us to manifest our desires more effectively. Heart coherence also enhances health and well-being, reducing stress, boosting immune function, and increasing emotional resilience.

The practice of heart coherence involves focusing on

the heart, breathing deeply and rhythmically, and cultivating positive emotions such as love, gratitude, and compassion. By regularly practicing heart coherence, we can strengthen the connection between the heart and mind, align ourselves with the divine, and create a more harmonious and fulfilling life.

The Heart as a Bridge Between Science and Spirituality

The heart's role as a bridge between science and spirituality exemplifies the unity of all things, the interconnectedness of the physical and spiritual, the seen and the unseen. The heart, with its powerful electromagnetic field, is a living demonstration of how the physical body is interwoven with the quantum field, how the material and the immaterial are inseparable aspects of the same reality.

In the realm of science, the heart's electromagnetic field is a measurable, quantifiable phenomenon, governed by the physical laws that structure the universe. In the realm of spirituality, the heart is a symbol of love, compassion, and unity, a reflection of the divine consciousness that permeates the cosmos. The heart is where these two realms converge, where science and spirituality dance in harmony and wholeness.

This convergence challenges us to view the heart not merely as a physical organ but as a multidimensional being, a nexus of energy and consciousness that transcends the boundaries of the physical world. It invites us to embrace the heart as a bridge between the physical and the spiritual, a gateway to higher consciousness, and a tool for creating a more harmonious and fulfilling life.

Harnessing the Quantum Heart for Spiritual Growth

The heart's electromagnetic field is a powerful tool for spiritual growth and transformation, a means by which we can influence the quantum field and shape the reality we experience. By cultivating heart coherence, aligning our emotions with the higher frequencies of love and compassion, and channelling our intentions through the heart, we can harness this power to create a life that reflects our highest aspirations and values.

The journey of harnessing the power of the quantum heart begins with a shift in awareness, a movement from the mind to the heart, from the intellectual to the intuitive, from the ego to the soul. This shift is not just a change in perspective; it is a transformation of consciousness, a movement from separation to unity, from fear to love, from limitation to infinity.

As we journey into the heart, we discover that the heart is not just a physical organ but a living, breathing expression of the divine. It is a bridge between the physical and the quantum realms, a gateway to higher consciousness, and a powerful tool for creating a life of love, compassion, and unity.

The Journey Into the Quantum Heart

As we conclude this chapter, we stand at the threshold of a new understanding of the heart, a deeper awareness of its role as a bridge between science and spirituality. The heart, with its powerful electromagnetic field, is not just a physical organ; it is a gateway to higher consciousness, a conduit through which we can influence the quantum field and shape the reality we experience.

The journey into the quantum heart is not merely a scientific inquiry or a spiritual exploration; it is a path of awakening that leads us to the heart of the divine. It invites us to recognize the heart's power to influence reality, to align our emotions with the higher frequencies of love and compassion, and to create a life that reflects our highest aspirations and values.

As we continue our journey into the heart of quantum spirituality, let us carry this awareness with us, allowing it to guide us in the dance of life. Let us recognize the quantum heart as a bridge between science and spirituality, a gateway to higher consciousness, and a powerful tool for creating a life of love, compassion, and unity.

The quantum heart is a profound bridge between science and spirituality, offering a deep understanding of how the heart's electromagnetic field influences reality. By harnessing the power of the quantum heart, we can align our emotions with the higher frequencies of love and compassion, access higher consciousness, and create a life that reflects our highest aspirations and values. As we delve into the deeper truths of quantum spirituality, we are invited to embrace the quantum heart as a gateway to the divine, a tool for spiritual growth, and a bridge between the physical and the spiritual realms.

CHAPTER 11: THE JOURNEY WITHIN- EXPLORING INNER REALMS THROUGH QUANTUM CONSCIOUSNESS

Introduction: The Quantum Mind as a Portal to the Inner Universe

As we journey deeper into the heart of quantum spirituality, we arrive at a threshold where the outer universe and the inner universe converge. This is the realm of quantum consciousness, where the mysteries of the cosmos mirror the mysteries of the self, and where the exploration of the quantum field becomes an exploration of our own inner landscape. In this chapter, inspired by the work of Stephen Wolinsky in "Quantum Consciousness," we embark on an inward journey, using the principles of quantum physics as a guide to explore the vast, uncharted territories of the mind and soul.

Quantum consciousness is not just a theoretical concept; it is a living, breathing reality that we can access through focused intention, meditation, and altered states of consciousness. By understanding and harnessing the principles of quantum mechanics, we can unlock the hidden potential within ourselves, access deeper levels of awareness, and experience profound spiritual awakening.

The Inner Universe: A Reflection of the Quantum Field

The concept of the inner universe is rooted in the idea that the mind is a microcosm of the macrocosm, a reflection of the quantum field that underlies all of reality. Just as the quantum field is a realm of infinite possibilities, where particles exist in a state of potential until observed, so too is the mind a field of potentialities, where thoughts, emotions, and beliefs shape the reality we experience.

In this view, the mind is not a passive receiver of information but an active participant in the creation of reality. Our thoughts and intentions interact with the quantum field, collapsing the wave function and bringing potentialities into actuality. This process is not limited to the physical world; it extends into the inner realms of consciousness, where our perceptions, beliefs, and emotions shape the landscape of the mind.

The inner universe is a vast, multidimensional space,

where the boundaries between self and other, subject and object, begin to dissolve. In this space, we can explore the deeper aspects of our being, connect with the higher dimensions of consciousness, and access the wisdom of the soul. The journey within is a journey into the heart of the quantum field, where the mysteries of the universe are mirrored in the mysteries of the self.

Altered States of Consciousness: Accessing the Quantum Mind

One of the most powerful ways to explore the inner universe is through altered states of consciousness—states where the ordinary boundaries of perception and awareness are expanded, allowing us to access deeper levels of the mind. These states can be induced through various practices, including meditation, deep relaxation, breathwork, and the use of certain plant medicines or entheogens.

In altered states of consciousness, the mind enters a state of heightened sensitivity and receptivity, where the ordinary filters of perception are loosened, and the deeper layers of the psyche are revealed. In this state, we can access the quantum mind—the aspect of consciousness that is directly connected to the quantum field, where all possibilities exist simultaneously.

In the quantum mind, the boundaries between self and other begin to blur, and the distinction between the inner and outer worlds dissolves. We enter a state of oneness, where we are no longer separate from the universe but are intimately connected with it. This state of unity consciousness is a direct experience of the quantum field, where the observer and the observed are one, and where the infinite potential of the universe is available to us.

The Quantum Leap: Transformation Through Inner Awareness

The journey within is not just an exploration of the inner universe; it is a journey of transformation—a quantum leap from the ordinary to the extraordinary, from the mundane to the sacred. In the quantum mind, we can experience profound shifts in consciousness, where old patterns of thought and behaviour are released, and new possibilities are brought into being.

This process of transformation is often accompanied by a deep sense of spiritual awakening, where we come to recognize our true nature as beings of consciousness, connected to the infinite intelligence of the universe. We realize that we are not separate from the world but are part of a larger, interconnected whole, and that our thoughts, emotions, and intentions have the power to shape reality.

The quantum leap is not just a change in perspective; it is a change in being—a shift from the ego-centred self to the soul-centred self, from the limited to the limitless, from the finite to the infinite. This transformation is not something that happens overnight; it is a gradual process of awakening, where we come to embody the higher frequencies of love, compassion, and unity, and where we align ourselves with the divine purpose of the soul.

The Practice of Quantum Meditation

One of the most effective ways to access the quantum mind and experience the quantum leap is through the practice of quantum meditation. Quantum meditation is a form of meditation that focuses on the principles of quantum consciousness, using the mind as a tool for exploring the inner universe and connecting with the quantum field.

In quantum meditation, we begin by focusing our awareness on the present moment, bringing our attention to the breath, and allowing the mind to become still and quiet. As we enter a state of deep relaxation, we shift our focus to the inner realms of consciousness, exploring the thoughts, emotions, and sensations that arise within us.

As we deepen our meditation, we begin to connect with the quantum mind, entering a state of oneness with the universe, where the boundaries between self and other dissolve. In this state, we can access the infinite potential of the quantum field, using our thoughts and intentions to shape the reality we experience.

Quantum meditation is not just a practice of relaxation; it is a practice of transformation, where we align ourselves with the higher frequencies of consciousness and experience the quantum leap from the ordinary to the extraordinary. Through regular practice, we can strengthen our connection with the quantum field, access deeper levels of awareness, and experience profound spiritual growth.

The Inner Journey: A Path to Spiritual Enlightenment

The journey within, guided by the principles of quantum consciousness, is a path to spiritual enlightenment—a journey that takes us beyond the limitations of the ego and the material world, into the higher dimensions of consciousness and the divine. In this journey, we come to realize that the outer universe reflects the inner universe, and that the path to spiritual awakening lies within us.

This inner journey is not just about exploring the mind; it is about experiencing the soul, the essence of who we are beyond the body and the mind. It is about connecting with the higher dimensions of consciousness, where we can access the wisdom, love, and light of the soul, and where we can experience the oneness of all life.

The path to spiritual enlightenment is not a linear journey; it is a spiral, where we continually deepen our understanding and awareness, moving closer to the centre of our being, the source of all life. Along this path, we encounter challenges and obstacles, but we also experience moments of profound insight and awakening, where we come to see the world and ourselves in a new light.

The journey within is a journey of self-discovery, where we come to know the true nature of who we are, and where we align ourselves with the divine purpose of the soul. It is a journey that requires courage, commitment, and a willingness to let go of old patterns and beliefs, but it is also a journey that brings us closer to the divine, and to the realization of our highest potential.

The Quantum Mind and the Future of Spirituality

As we explore the quantum mind and the journey within, we are also exploring the future of spirituality —a future where science and spirituality are no longer separate but are united in a common quest for truth and understanding. The principles of quantum consciousness offer us a new paradigm for spirituality, one that is based on the interconnectedness of all life, the power of consciousness to shape reality, and the infinite potential of the soul.

In this new paradigm, spirituality is not just a set of beliefs or practices, but a way of being, a way of living in alignment with the higher dimensions of consciousness and the divine. It is a way of recognizing the sacredness of all life, and of using our thoughts, emotions, and intentions to create a world that reflects the highest ideals of love, compassion, and unity.

The quantum mind offers us a powerful tool for spiritual growth and transformation, a means by which we can access the deeper dimensions of consciousness and experience the oneness of all life. It invites us to move beyond the limitations of the ego and the material world, and to embrace the infinite potential of the soul, the divine essence that lies within each of us.

The Journey Continues: Embracing the Quantum Mind

As we conclude this chapter, we stand at the threshold of a new understanding of spirituality, a new awareness of the quantum mind and its role in the journey within. The quantum mind is not just a theoretical concept; it is a living, breathing reality, a reflection of the infinite potential of the universe and the soul.

The journey within is a journey of self-discovery, a path to spiritual enlightenment, and a means by which we can align ourselves with the higher dimensions of consciousness and the divine. It is a journey that takes us beyond the limitations of the ego and the material world, into the heart of the quantum field, where all possibilities exist.

As we continue our journey into the heart of quantum spirituality, let us carry this awareness with us, and let it guide us in the dance of life. Let us embrace the quantum mind as a tool for spiritual growth and transformation and let us use it to create a life that reflects the highest ideals of love, compassion, and unity.

The journey within, guided by the principles of quantum consciousness, offers a profound path to spiritual enlightenment. By exploring the inner universe and accessing the quantum mind, we can experience the oneness of all life, align ourselves with the divine, and create a life that reflects our highest aspirations. As we explore the deeper truths of quantum spirituality, we are invited to embrace the quantum mind as a gateway to the infinite potential of the soul and the divine.

CHAPTER 12: THE MYSTICAL QUANTUM: BEYOND THE MATERIAL WORLD

In the shadowed depths of the cosmos, where the tangible dissolves into the intangible and the known merges with the unknown, lies a reality that defies the ordinary bounds of perception. This is the mystical quantum—a realm where the material world is but a veil, thin and translucent, through which we can glimpse the infinite and the eternal. Inspired by Michael Talbot's Mysticism and the New Physics, this chapter explores the profound intersection between quantum physics and mysticism, offering a doorway to realms beyond the physical, where the sacred and the scientific converge in a dance of mystery and revelation.

The Quantum Veil: Seeing Beyond the Material World

Quantum physics, with its strange and paradoxical principles, has opened a doorway to a deeper understanding of reality—one that transcends the limits of the material world. In the quantum realm, particles exist in a state of superposition, where they can be in multiple places at once, and where their properties are not fixed until observed. This challenges the classical view of a deterministic, objective universe and suggests that reality is far more fluid and interconnected than we have traditionally believed.

This quantum reality is not confined to the world of particles; it extends into the very fabric of existence, offering a glimpse beyond the material world into a realm that is both mystical and profound. In this realm, the boundaries between subject and object, self and other, dissolve, revealing a universe that is deeply interconnected and alive with possibilities.

The idea that the material world is but a veil, concealing a deeper, more fundamental reality, is a theme that runs through many mystical traditions. Mystics throughout history have spoken of a reality beyond the physical, a realm of pure consciousness, where the material world is seen as an illusion or a shadow of a higher truth. Quantum physics, in its exploration of the subatomic world, offers a scientific framework for understanding these mystical insights, suggesting that the material world is not the ultimate reality, but a manifestation of a deeper, quantum field of potential.

Mystical Experiences and Quantum Reality

Mystical experiences—those moments of profound insight, unity, and transcendence—offer a direct experience of this deeper reality. These experiences often involve a sense of oneness with the universe, where the boundaries of the self-dissolve, and the individual consciousness merges with the infinite. In this state, the ordinary distinctions between the material and the spiritual, the physical and the metaphysical, disappear, revealing a reality that is boundless, timeless, and infinitely interconnected.

Quantum physics provides a framework for understanding these mystical experiences, suggesting that they are not merely subjective states of mind, but reflections of a deeper, quantum reality. In the quantum realm, the concept of nonlocality suggests that particles can be instantaneously connected across vast distances, defying the limitations of space and time. This phenomenon is akin to the mystical experience of unity, where the boundaries of space and time are transcended, and the individual consciousness is connected to the whole.

The idea that consciousness itself is a fundamental aspect of reality is a theme that runs through both quantum physics and mysticism. In the mystical traditions, consciousness is seen as the ground of being, the source from which all things arise, and the medium through which the universe is perceived. Quantum physics, with its emphasis on the role of the observer in shaping reality, echoes this idea, suggesting that consciousness is not just a passive observer of the world, but an active participant in its creation.

The Quantum Mysticism of Nonlocality and Entanglement

One of the most intriguing aspects of quantum physics is the phenomenon of nonlocality—the idea that particles can be instantaneously connected, regardless of the distance between them. This phenomenon, known as quantum entanglement, suggests that the universe is deeply interconnected, and that the actions of one particle can influence another, even if they are light-years apart.

This concept of nonlocality resonates with the mystical idea of the interconnectedness of all things—a fundamental principle in many spiritual traditions. Mystics have long taught that all of creation is interconnected, that the universe is a web of relationships where every part is connected to every other part. Quantum entanglement provides a scientific framework for understanding this mystical insight, suggesting that the universe is indeed a unified whole, where all things are connected in ways that transcend the limitations of space and time.

In the mystical experience, this interconnectedness is often felt as a deep sense of unity, where the self is no longer separate from the world, but is part of a larger, interconnected whole. This experience of unity is not just a psychological state; it reflects the deeper reality that quantum physics reveals—a reality where all things are connected in a web of relationships that transcends the physical.

The phenomenon of quantum entanglement also

suggests that the universe is not a collection of isolated objects, but a unified field of energy and information, where the actions of one part can influence the whole. This idea is central to many mystical traditions, which teach that the universe is a living, conscious entity, and that every action, thought, and intention has an impact on the whole.

The Role of Consciousness in Shaping Reality

In both quantum physics and mysticism, consciousness plays a central role in shaping reality. In the quantum realm, the observer effect suggests that the act of observation collapses the wave function, bringing potentialities into actuality. This implies that consciousness is not just a passive observer of reality, but an active participant in its creation.

This idea is echoed in the mystical traditions, which teach that consciousness is the ground of being, the source from which all things arise. In this view, the world we perceive reflects our consciousness, a manifestation of the thoughts, beliefs, and intentions we hold within our minds. The material world is not separate from consciousness, but is shaped by it, just as the quantum field is shaped by the observer.

The idea that consciousness shapes reality challenges the traditional, materialistic view of the universe, which sees the world as a collection of separate, independent objects. Instead, it suggests that reality is a dynamic, interconnected process, where consciousness and matter are inseparable aspects of the same whole.

This understanding of consciousness as a fundamental

aspect of reality has profound implications for our understanding of the self and the universe. It suggests that we are not separate from the world, but are intimately connected to it, and that our thoughts, emotions, and intentions have the power to shape the reality we experience.

The Mystical Path: Awakening to the Quantum Reality

The exploration of the mystical quantum is not just an intellectual pursuit; it is a path of awakening—a journey into the deeper dimensions of reality, where the boundaries of the material world dissolve, and the sacred is revealed. This path invites us to move beyond the limitations of the ego and the material world, and to awaken to the deeper reality that lies beyond the veil of the physical.

In this journey, we are called to explore the mystical aspects of our own consciousness, to access the deeper dimensions of the mind, and to experience the unity of all life. This exploration is not just a psychological or spiritual process; it is a quantum leap—a shift in consciousness that takes us beyond the ordinary, into the realm of the extraordinary.

The mystical path is a journey of transformation, where we move from the limited, ego-centred self to the expanded, soul-centred self, from the finite to the infinite, from the material to the spiritual. Along this path, we encounter the deeper truths of existence, the mysteries of the quantum field, and the sacred geometry of the universe.

This journey is not without its challenges. The mystical

path requires us to confront the illusions of the material world, to let go of old patterns and beliefs, and to embrace the unknown. But it is also a journey of profound insight and awakening, where we come to see the world and ourselves in a new light.

The Quantum Mysticism of Love and Unity

At the heart of the mystical path is the experience of love and unity—a fundamental principle in both quantum physics and mysticism. In the quantum realm, the interconnectedness of all things is reflected in the phenomenon of quantum entanglement, where particles remain connected across vast distances, regardless of space and time. In the mystical experience, this interconnectedness is felt as a deep sense of love and unity, where the self is no longer separate from the world, but is part of a larger, interconnected whole.

This experience of love and unity is not just an emotional state; it reflects the deeper reality that quantum physics reveals—a reality where all things are connected in a web of relationships that transcend the physical. In this state of unity consciousness, we experience the oneness of all life, the interconnectedness of the universe, and the profound love that binds all things together.

The mystical experience of love and unity is a direct experience of the quantum field, where the boundaries of space and time dissolve, and the infinite potential of the universe is available to us. In this state, we come to realize that we are not separate from the world, but are part of a larger, interconnected whole, and that our thoughts, emotions, and intentions have the power to shape reality.

The Future of Quantum Mysticism

As we explore the mystical aspects of quantum physics, we are also exploring the future of spirituality—a future where science and spirituality are no longer separate but are united in a common quest for truth and understanding. The principles of quantum mysticism offer us a new paradigm for spirituality, one that is based on the interconnectedness of all life, the power of consciousness to shape reality, and the infinite potential of the soul.

In this new paradigm, spirituality is not just a set of beliefs or practices, but a way of being, a way of living in alignment with the higher dimensions of consciousness and the divine. It is a way of recognizing the sacredness of all life, and of using our thoughts, emotions, and intentions to create a world that reflects the highest ideals of love, compassion, and unity.

Quantum mysticism offers us a powerful tool for spiritual growth and transformation, a means by which we can access the deeper dimensions of consciousness and experience the oneness of all life. It invites us to move beyond the limitations of the ego and the material world, and to embrace the infinite potential of the soul, the divine essence that lies within each of us.

The Journey Beyond the Material World

As we conclude this chapter, we find ourselves standing at the threshold of a new understanding of reality, a new awareness of the mystical quantum and its role in shaping our experience of the world. The mystical quantum is not just a scientific concept; it reflects the deeper reality that lies beyond the material world, a realm where the sacred and the scientific converge in a dance of mystery and revelation.

The journey beyond the material world is a journey of awakening, where we move from the limited, ego-centred self to the expanded, soul-centred self, from the finite to the infinite, from the material to the spiritual. It is a journey that takes us beyond the ordinary, into the realm of the extraordinary, where the mysteries of the quantum field are revealed, and the sacred geometry of the universe is experienced.

As we continue our journey into the heart of quantum spirituality, let us carry this awareness with us, and let it guide us in the dance of life. Let us embrace the mystical quantum as a tool for spiritual growth and transformation and let us use it to create a life that reflects the highest ideals of love, compassion, and unity.

The mystical quantum offers a profound glimpse beyond the material world, revealing the deeper reality that lies at the heart of existence. By exploring the intersection of quantum physics and mysticism, we can experience the oneness of all life, align ourselves with the divine, and create a life that reflects our highest aspirations. As we delve into the deeper truths of quantum spirituality, we are invited to embrace the mystical quantum as a gateway to the infinite potential of the soul and the divine.

CHAPTER 13: THE SACRED ECHO: RESONATING WITH THE DIVINE THROUGH QUANTUM UNDERSTANDING

In the silent spaces between the beats of existence, where the unseen ripples of reality pulse through the cosmos, there lies a profound truth—a truth that resonates with the very fabric of creation. This is the sacred echo, a reverberation of the divine will that flows through the quantum wave function, shaping the dance of particles and the unfolding of the universe. Inspired by Norman Friedman's The Hidden Domain, this chapter explores the idea that the quantum wave function is not merely a mathematical abstraction, but a sacred echo of divine intention, guiding us towards a deeper connection with the sacred and a more harmonious existence.

The Quantum Wave Function: A Sacred Resonance

At the heart of quantum mechanics lies the concept of the wave function—a mathematical expression that describes the probabilities of a quantum system's various possible states. The wave function is a complex entity, existing not in the physical world we see but in an abstract, multidimensional space. It embodies the potentialities of a system, a realm of pure possibility before anything becomes actualized.

But what if this wave function is more than just a tool for physicists? What if it is, in essence, a sacred resonance—a subtle, divine melody that sings the universe into being? In this view, the quantum wave function is not just a probabilistic description; it is the very echo of the divine will, the blueprint by which the cosmos is formed and maintained.

This sacred echo permeates all levels of existence, from the smallest subatomic particle to the vast expanse of galaxies. It is the underlying vibration that holds the universe together, a resonance that reflects the divine intention in every atom, every star, and every thought. To understand the wave function in this way is to glimpse the interconnectedness of all things and to see the hand of the divine in the workings of the quantum world.

Resonating with the Divine: Aligning with the Sacred Echo

To resonate with the divine is to align oneself with this sacred echo, to attune one's consciousness to the subtle vibrations that underpin reality. This alignment is not just a metaphysical concept; it is a practical and profound way of being, a path to greater harmony, peace, and fulfilment in life.

Resonance, in the physical sense, occurs when one system vibrates in harmony with another. In the context of quantum spirituality, it means tuning our inner frequencies—our thoughts, emotions, and intentions—to the frequencies of the quantum wave function, the divine blueprint that shapes reality. When we align our consciousness with this sacred resonance, we become co-creators with the divine, participating in the ongoing act of creation.

This process of alignment requires us to cultivate awareness and mindfulness, to become attuned to the subtle energies that flow through us and around us. It involves quieting the mind, opening the heart, and listening deeply to the inner voice of the soul—the voice that resonates with the sacred echo. In doing so, we begin to live in harmony with the divine will, allowing the wave function to guide our actions, our decisions, and our lives.

The Harmony of the Spheres: A Cosmic Symphony

The concept of resonance has deep roots in both science and mysticism. In ancient times, philosophers spoke of the Harmony of the Spheres—the idea that the planets and stars move in a cosmic symphony, creating a music that reflects the order and harmony of the universe. This music, though inaudible to the human ear, was believed to influence the soul and the natural world, a divine resonance that held the cosmos in balance.

In the quantum realm, this harmony is reflected in the wave function, which describes the coherent, orderly behaviour of particles in a quantum system. When particles are in resonance, they move in harmony with one another, creating patterns of interference that reveal the underlying order of the quantum field. This is not just a physical phenomenon; it reflects the divine order that pervades the universe, a sacred geometry that shapes the dance of creation.

The Harmony of the Spheres is more than a poetic metaphor; it is a profound truth that speaks to the interconnectedness of all things. Just as the planets and stars move in harmony with one another, so too can we move in harmony with the quantum field, resonating with the divine will and aligning ourselves with the cosmic symphony that holds the universe together.

The Role of Consciousness in Shaping Reality

In the quantum realm, consciousness plays a crucial role in shaping reality. The wave function, with all its potentialities, collapses into a single outcome when observed—this is the essence of the observer effect. But this collapse is not random; it is guided by the consciousness of the observer, by the thoughts, beliefs, and intentions that shape our perception of the world.

When we align our consciousness with the sacred echo of the wave function, we participate in the act of creation, shaping reality in accordance with the divine will. This is a profound responsibility, for it means that our thoughts and intentions have the power to influence the world around us, to bring into being the possibilities that resonate with our deepest desires and highest aspirations.

This understanding challenges us to cultivate a deeper awareness of our thoughts and emotions, to become mindful of the vibrations we are sending into the quantum field. By aligning our consciousness with the sacred echo, we can create a life that is in harmony with the divine, a life that reflects the beauty, order, and unity of the cosmos.

The Path of Resonance: Living in Harmony with the Divine

Living in harmony with the divine is not just about aligning our consciousness with the quantum wave function; it is about embodying the principles of resonance in every aspect of our lives. It is about living in a way that reflects the unity of all things, the interconnectedness of the cosmos, and the sacredness of existence.

This path of resonance invites us to cultivate love, compassion, and gratitude, to attune our hearts to the higher frequencies of the divine. It challenges us to let go of fear, anger, and resentment, to release the lower vibrations that create dissonance in our lives and in the world. By doing so, we create a harmonious field of energy that resonates with the sacred echo, attracting into our lives the experiences, relationships, and opportunities that reflect our highest good.

The path of resonance is also a path of service, a commitment to living in a way that benefits others and the world as a whole. When we resonate with the divine, we become channels for the flow of love and light, bringing healing, peace, and harmony to those around us. This is not just a personal journey; it is a collective one, a call to awaken to our interconnectedness and to contribute to the creation of a more harmonious and compassionate world.

The Sacred Echo in Everyday Life

The sacred echo is not just a concept to be contemplated; it is a reality to be experienced in every moment of our lives. By tuning into this resonance, we can bring the divine into our daily existence, creating a life that is infused with meaning, purpose, and joy.

This involves cultivating a practice of mindfulness, being present to the subtle energies that flow through us and around us. It means listening to the inner voice of the soul, the whisper of the divine that guides us on our path. It also involves making choices that are in alignment with our highest values and deepest truths, creating a life that resonates with the sacred echo.

In practical terms, this might mean starting the day with a meditation that aligns our consciousness with the divine, setting intentions that resonate with our highest aspirations, and making decisions that reflect our commitment to living in harmony with the sacred. It might also involve practices such as gratitude, which helps to attune our hearts to the higher frequencies of love and compassion, and service, which allows us to bring the divine into the world through our actions.

The Journey of Resonance: Embracing the Sacred Echo

As we conclude this chapter, we are invited to embrace the sacred echo as a guiding principle in our lives. The quantum wave function, with its infinite potentialities, reflects the divine will, a sacred resonance that shapes the dance of creation. By aligning ourselves with this resonance, we can live in harmony with the divine, creating a life that reflects the beauty, order, and unity of the cosmos.

This journey of resonance is not just a path of spiritual growth; it is a way of being, a way of living in alignment with the divine. It invites us to attune our consciousness to the subtle vibrations that flow through the quantum field, to listen to the sacred echo that guides us on our path, and to create a life that resonates with the highest frequencies of love, compassion, and unity.

As we continue our journey into the heart of quantum spirituality, let us carry this awareness with us, and let it guide us in the dance of life. Let us resonate with the sacred echo, aligning ourselves with the divine will, and creating a life that reflects the infinite potential of the soul and the cosmos.

The sacred echo, as reflected in the quantum wave function, offers a profound understanding of the interconnectedness of all things and our role in the creation of reality. By resonating with this divine resonance, we can align ourselves with the higher frequencies of love, compassion, and unity, creating a life that is in harmony with the divine. As we explore the deeper truths of quantum spirituality, we are invited to embrace the sacred echo as a guiding principle, living in resonance with the divine will and contributing to the creation of a more harmonious and compassionate world.

CHAPTER 14: THE QUANTUM PILGRIMAGE: A SPIRITUAL QUEST THROUGH SCIENCE

In the twilight realm where the ancient wisdom of the mystic converges with the cutting-edge revelations of the physicist, there unfolds a journey —a pilgrimage not of mere physical travel, but of the soul's awakening through the vast landscapes of both the seen and the unseen. This is the quantum pilgrimage, a profound and transformative odyssey that merges the rigors of scientific inquiry with the profundities of spiritual discovery. Inspired by The Quantum and the Lotus by Matthieu Ricard and Trinh Xuan Thuan, this chapter invites you to embark on this sacred journey, where the quantum world becomes the map, and the soul's longing for truth becomes the compass.

The Convergence of Science and Spirituality: A New Pathway

In an era where science often stands as the bastion of rationality and spirituality as the sanctuary of the ineffable, there arises a unique opportunity—a convergence where these two seemingly disparate paths intertwine, revealing a deeper, unified truth. The quantum pilgrimage is a pathway through this convergence, a journey that does not seek to diminish the distinctions between science and spirituality, but rather to integrate them, recognizing that each offers a vital perspective on the nature of reality.

The journey begins with the recognition that science and spirituality are not enemies, but allies in the search for truth. Science, with its empirical methods and logical frameworks, seeks to understand the mechanics of the universe—the show of existence. Spirituality, with its emphasis on inner experience and transcendence, seeks to understand the meaning of the universe—the why of existence. Together, they form a holistic approach to the great questions of life, offering not just knowledge, but wisdom.

In this context, the quantum pilgrimage is a journey of integration, where the insights of quantum physics illuminate the ancient teachings of the mystics, and where the practices of spirituality deepen our understanding of the quantum world. It is a journey that leads us to the heart of reality, where the material and the immaterial, the physical and the metaphysical, meet in a dance of harmony and unity.

The Quantum World as a Sacred Map

The quantum world, with its bewildering principles and paradoxical phenomena, offers a map for the spiritual pilgrim—one that guides us through the labyrinth of existence, revealing the hidden connections that bind all things together. At the heart of this map is the concept of nonlocality, the idea that particles, once entangled, remain connected across vast distances, regardless of space and time. This phenomenon challenges our traditional notions of separateness and individuality, suggesting instead that the universe is a unified whole, where everything is interconnected in a web of relationships.

In the quantum pilgrimage, nonlocality becomes a metaphor for the interconnectedness of all life, a reminder that we are not isolated beings, but part of a greater whole. This understanding invites us to expand our sense of self, to see ourselves not as separate entities, but as threads in the vast tapestry of existence. It encourages us to cultivate compassion and empathy, recognizing that what we do to others, we do to ourselves, for in the quantum realm, all actions reverberate across the entire cosmos.

Another key concept in the quantum world is the observer effect, which suggests that the act of observation influences the outcome of an experiment. In the quantum pilgrimage, this principle becomes a powerful tool for spiritual growth, teaching us that our perceptions, thoughts, and intentions shape the reality we experience. By becoming conscious observers of our own lives, we can influence the unfolding of our destiny, aligning our actions with the deeper currents of the quantum field.

The Spiritual Practices of the Quantum Pilgrim

The quantum pilgrimage is not merely a conceptual journey; it is a lived experience, one that requires the pilgrim to engage in practices that bridge the gap between science and spirituality. These practices are not about abandoning one's rational faculties in favour of blind faith, nor are they about reducing spiritual experiences to mere scientific phenomena. Rather, they are about integrating the insights of both paths, creating a holistic approach to the journey of the soul.

Meditative Inquiry: At the heart of the quantum pilgrimage is the practice of meditative inquiry—a fusion of meditation and intellectual exploration. This practice involves entering a state of deep meditation, where the mind becomes still and receptive, and then contemplating the principles of quantum physics in light of spiritual teachings. For example, one might meditate on the concept of nonlocality, exploring how this principle reflects the interconnectedness of all life, or on the observer effect, contemplating how our thoughts shape reality. This practice not only deepens one's understanding of quantum principles but also integrates them into the fabric of one's spiritual life.

Quantum Visualization: Another powerful practice is quantum visualization, a technique that involves using the imagination to interact with the quantum field. In this practice, the pilgrim visualizes the quantum world, seeing themselves as a part of the intricate web of relationships that connect all things. They might imagine the quantum field as a sea of potentialities, where every thought, emotion, and action sends ripples across the cosmos, influencing the unfolding of reality. By visualizing themselves as a conscious participant in this field, the pilgrim can cultivate a sense of agency and responsibility, recognizing that they have the power to shape their destiny through their intentions and actions.

Contemplative Science: The quantum pilgrimage also involves the practice of contemplative science, a way of approaching scientific inquiry with a sense of reverence and awe. In this practice, the pilgrim studies the discoveries of quantum physics not merely as intellectual concepts, but as sacred revelations—glimpses into the divine order that underlies the universe. Contemplative science is about seeing the study of the natural world as a spiritual practice, one that brings us closer to the divine by revealing the intricate and harmonious patterns of creation.

Embodying the Quantum Mindset: Finally, the quantum pilgrimage requires the pilgrim to embody the quantum mindset—a way of being that is open, flexible, and attuned to the mysteries of the universe. This mindset involves embracing uncertainty and paradox, recognizing that the universe is not a fixed and predictable machine, but a dynamic and evolving process. It requires the pilgrim to cultivate humility, knowing that our understanding of reality is always partial and provisional, and to approach the world with a sense of wonder and curiosity, always open to new possibilities and deeper insights.

The Inner and Outer Pilgrimage: Journeying Through Mind and World

The quantum pilgrimage is both an inner and an outer journey—an exploration of the depths of the mind and the expanses of the world. It involves traveling through the landscapes of consciousness, where the boundaries between self and other dissolve, and the mysteries of the quantum field are revealed. It also involves engaging with the physical world, where the principles of quantum physics manifest in the patterns of nature, the movements of the stars, and the dynamics of everyday life.

On the inner journey, the pilgrim explores the quantum dimensions of the mind, delving into the subconscious realms where thoughts and emotions take shape, and where the seeds of intention are planted. This journey is about becoming aware of the subtle energies that flow through the mind and learning to direct these energies in ways that align with the deeper truths of the quantum field. It is about cultivating a sense of inner harmony, where the mind becomes a reflection of the cosmic order, and where the sacred echo of the quantum wave function resonates within the soul.

On the outer journey, the pilgrim engages with the world in a way that reflects the principles of quantum spirituality. This involves seeing the world not as a collection of separate objects, but as a unified field of energy and consciousness, where everything is interconnected and interdependent. It involves acting with awareness and intention, knowing that every action sends ripples across the quantum field, influencing the unfolding of reality. And it involves living in harmony with the natural world, recognizing that the patterns of nature are reflections of the divine order that underlies the universe.

The Pilgrim's Gift: Bringing the Sacred Into the World

The quantum pilgrimage is not just a journey for the sake of personal enlightenment; it is a journey that seeks to bring the sacred into the world, to infuse everyday life with the insights and wisdom gained along the way. The pilgrim's gift is the ability to see the world through the lens of quantum spirituality, to recognize the sacredness of all things, and to live in a way that reflects this recognition.

This gift is about bringing the principles of quantum physics into the realm of everyday life, using them to guide our thoughts, actions, and relationships. It is about seeing every moment as an opportunity to resonate with the divine, to align our consciousness with the sacred echo of the quantum wave function, and to create a life that reflects the beauty, harmony, and unity of the cosmos.

The pilgrim's gift is also about sharing the insights and wisdom gained on the journey with others, helping to awaken them to the deeper realities that underlie the material world. It is about fostering a sense of community, where the principles of quantum spirituality are lived and practiced, creating a collective field of resonance that amplifies the sacred echo and brings about positive change in the world.

The Quantum Pilgrimage as a Lifelong Journey

The quantum pilgrimage is not a journey with a fixed destination; it is a lifelong quest, one that continues to unfold as we grow and evolve. It is a journey that invites us to continually deepen our understanding of the quantum world and to integrate its principles into our spiritual practice. It is a journey that challenges us to remain open and curious, always seeking new insights and deeper truths, and to live in a way that reflects the sacredness of all things.

As we walk this path, we are reminded that the quantum pilgrimage is not just a solitary journey; it is a collective one, where we walk alongside others who share our quest for truth and understanding. Together, we create a field of resonance that amplifies the sacred echo, bringing the divine into the world and helping to create a more harmonious and compassionate society.

The quantum pilgrimage is a journey of integration, where science and spirituality come together in a dance of harmony and unity. It is a journey that takes us to the heart of reality, where the material and the immaterial, the physical and the metaphysical, meet in a sacred convergence. And it is a journey that invites us to live in resonance with the divine, creating a life that reflects the beauty, harmony, and unity of the cosmos.

The Sacred Path: A Call to the Quantum Pilgrimage

As we conclude this chapter, we stand at the threshold of the quantum pilgrimage, ready to embark on a journey that will take us beyond the boundaries of the known, into the mysteries of the unknown. This journey is not just about understanding the quantum world; it is about experiencing it, living it, and embodying its principles in every aspect of our lives.

The quantum pilgrimage is a call to integrate the insights

of science with the wisdom of spirituality, to create a path that leads to deeper understanding, greater harmony, and a more profound connection with the divine. It is a call to resonate with the sacred echo, to align our consciousness with the divine will, and to create a life that reflects the infinite potential of the soul and the cosmos.

As we step onto this path, let us carry with us the awareness that the quantum pilgrimage is not just a journey for ourselves, but for the world. It is a journey that seeks to bring the sacred into everyday life, to create a world that reflects the highest ideals of love, compassion, and unity, and to resonate with the divine in all that we do.

The quantum pilgrimage is a profound journey that merges scientific inquiry with spiritual discovery, offering a path of integration that leads to deeper understanding, greater harmony, and a more profound connection with the divine. By embracing the principles of quantum physics and integrating them into our spiritual practice, we can create a life that resonates with the sacred echo, bringing the divine into the world and creating a life that reflects the beauty, harmony, and unity of the cosmos.

CHAPTER 15: THE DIVINE BLUEPRINT: UNDERSTANDING LIFE'S PURPOSE THROUGH QUANTUM PRINCIPLES

I n the ethereal lattice of the cosmos, where the dance of particles and the whisper of angels intertwine, there exists a blueprint—a divine design that weaves together the threads of existence into a tapestry of meaning and purpose. This is the divine blueprint, an intricate plan encoded in the quantum field, where the physical and spiritual realms converge to reveal the deeper truths of our lives. Inspired by The Physics of Angels by Matthew Fox and Rupert Sheldrake, this chapter explores how quantum principles can guide us in uncovering the divine blueprint that shapes our destinies and how we can align with this sacred pattern to fulfil our highest purpose.

The Cosmic Architecture: A Divine Blueprint in the Quantum Field

The notion of a divine blueprint is an ancient one, found in spiritual traditions that speak of a higher order, a cosmic architecture that governs the unfolding of the universe. In these traditions, this blueprint is often seen as a divine plan, a sacred design that reflects the will of the Creator and guides the evolution of all beings. In the context of quantum spirituality, this blueprint is encoded in the quantum field—the fundamental fabric of reality where all possibilities exist, and where the divine plan is woven into the very structure of existence.

The quantum field, with its infinite potentialities and interconnectedness, is not a random or chaotic space; it is a realm of order and harmony, where the divine blueprint is expressed through the patterns and processes of the cosmos. This blueprint is not a rigid or deterministic plan, but a dynamic and evolving design, one that allows for creativity, free will, and the unfolding of unique destinies. It is a living blueprint, one that resonates with the sacred echo of the divine will and guides the flow of energy and information throughout the universe.

In this view, the divine blueprint is not something external to us, imposed upon us by a distant deity; it is something that is intimately connected to our own being, encoded in the very fabric of our consciousness.

Just as the quantum field is a field of possibilities, so too is our consciousness a field of potential, where the divine blueprint can be accessed, understood, and realized through our thoughts, intentions, and actions.

The Role of Quantum Principles in Revealing Life's Purpose

Quantum principles offer a profound framework for understanding the divine blueprint and its role in shaping our lives. One of the key principles is that of superposition, which suggests that particles exist in multiple states simultaneously until they are observed. In the context of the divine blueprint, superposition represents the potentialities of our lives—the myriad possibilities that exist within the quantum field, waiting to be actualized through our choices and actions.

This principle challenges the idea of a fixed or predetermined destiny, suggesting instead that our lives are a dynamic interplay of possibilities, where the divine blueprint offers a range of potential paths, each leading to different outcomes. Our purpose is not something that is set in stone; it is something that we co-create with the divine, through the choices we make and the intentions we set.

Another key quantum principle is entanglement, which reveals the interconnectedness of all things. In the context of the divine blueprint, entanglement reflects the idea that our lives are not isolated or separate from the rest of the universe, but are part of a larger, interconnected whole. Our purpose is not just about fulfilling our own desires or ambitions; it is about contributing to the greater good, aligning our individual blueprint with the cosmic blueprint that guides the evolution of all beings.

This principle invites us to expand our understanding of purpose, to see it not just as a personal goal or achievement, but as a contribution to the harmony and balance of the universe. It challenges us to consider how our actions affect others, how our choices resonate through the quantum field, influencing the unfolding of reality in ways that we may not fully comprehend.

Accessing the Divine Blueprint Through Spiritual Practices

While the divine blueprint is encoded in the quantum field, it is not something that can be accessed through intellectual understanding alone. It requires a deep connection to the spiritual dimensions of our being, a receptivity to the subtle energies and patterns that flow through the quantum field. This connection can be cultivated through various spiritual practices that help us attune to the divine blueprint and align our lives with its sacred design.

Meditation is one of the most powerful practices for accessing the divine blueprint. In meditation, we quiet the mind and open the heart, creating a space where the subtle vibrations of the quantum field can be felt and understood. Through meditation, we can connect with the deeper layers of our consciousness, where the divine blueprint is encoded, and receive insights and guidance that help us navigate our lives in alignment with our higher purpose.

Visualization is another practice that can help us attune

to the divine blueprint. By visualizing our lives as part of a larger, cosmic design, we can begin to see how our individual purpose fits into the greater whole. Visualization allows us to explore the possibilities that exist within the quantum field, to see the different paths that are available to us, and to choose the one that resonates most deeply with our soul's calling.

Prayer is a practice that connects us with the divine will, opening a channel of communication between our consciousness and the higher dimensions of the quantum field. Through prayer, we can ask for guidance, seek clarity on our purpose, and align our intentions with the divine blueprint. Prayer is not just a request for help; it is a dialogue with the divine, a way of tuning into the sacred frequencies that guide the unfolding of our lives.

Sacred Rituals can also help us connect with the divine blueprint, by creating a space where the sacred and the mundane meet, where the quantum field and the physical world are brought into alignment. Rituals such as lighting a candle, offering a prayer, or creating an altar can help us attune to the divine blueprint, reminding us of the sacredness of our lives and the importance of living in harmony with the cosmic order.

The Divine Blueprint and the Purpose of Life

The divine blueprint offers a profound understanding of the purpose of life, revealing that our lives are not random or meaningless, but are part of a larger, sacred design. This purpose is not just about achieving success, acquiring wealth, or gaining recognition; it is about fulfilling the unique role that we were created to play in the unfolding of the universe.

Our purpose is encoded in the quantum field, woven into the fabric of our consciousness, and revealed through the choices we make and the paths we follow. It is not something that we have to discover or create from scratch; it is something that we have to remember, reconnect with, and to align ourselves with through our thoughts, intentions, and actions.

The purpose of life is not a fixed or static goal; it is a dynamic and evolving process, one that unfolds as we grow, learn, and evolve. It is a journey of self-discovery, where we come to understand who we are, why we are here, and how we can contribute to the greater good. It is a journey that requires us to listen to the inner voice of the soul, to follow the guidance of the divine blueprint, and to live in harmony with the sacred order of the cosmos.

Living in Alignment with the Divine Blueprint

Living in alignment with the divine blueprint is not just about following a set of rules or adhering to a specific doctrine; it is about living in a way that reflects the sacredness of our lives and the interconnectedness of all things. It is about cultivating a sense of reverence for the quantum field, recognizing that it is not just a physical phenomenon, but a manifestation of the divine will, a sacred space where the blueprint of our lives is woven into the fabric of the cosmos.

To live in alignment with the divine blueprint, we must cultivate awareness and mindfulness, becoming attuned to the subtle energies that flow through the quantum field and guide the unfolding of our lives. We must listen to the inner voice of the soul, the whisper of the divine that speaks to us through our thoughts, feelings, and intuitions, guiding us towards our highest purpose.

This alignment requires us to live with integrity, to act in ways that are consistent with our deepest values and highest aspirations. It challenges us to let go of ego-driven desires and attachments, to release the need for control, and to trust in the divine order that governs the universe. It invites us to live with an open heart, embracing love, compassion, and kindness as the guiding principles of our lives.

Living in alignment with the divine blueprint is also about being of service to others, recognizing that our purpose is not just about fulfilling our desires, but about contributing to the greater good. It is about using our gifts, talents, and abilities to make a positive impact on the world, to bring healing, peace, and harmony to those around us, and to help create a more just and compassionate society.

The Journey of Alignment: Embracing the Divine Blueprint

As we conclude this chapter, we are invited to embrace the divine blueprint as the guiding force in our lives, to align ourselves with the sacred design that shapes our destinies and to live in harmony with the cosmic order that governs the universe. The divine blueprint is not just a concept to be understood; it is a reality to be experienced, a path to be followed, and a purpose to be fulfilled.

The journey of alignment is not always easy; it requires

us to confront our fears, doubts, and insecurities, to let go of old patterns and beliefs, and to embrace the unknown. But it is also a journey of profound discovery and transformation, where we come to understand the deeper meaning of our lives, the unique role we were created to play, and the infinite potential that lies within us.

As we continue our journey into the heart of quantum spirituality, let us carry this awareness with us, and let it guide us in the dance of life. Let us embrace the divine blueprint as the sacred design that shapes our destinies, and let us live in alignment with its principles, creating a life that reflects the beauty, harmony, and unity of the cosmos.

The divine blueprint offers a profound understanding of life's purpose, revealing that our lives are part of a larger, sacred design that is encoded in the quantum field. By aligning ourselves with this blueprint, we can fulfil our highest purpose, living in harmony with the divine will and contributing to the greater good. As we explore the deeper truths of quantum spirituality, we are invited to embrace the divine blueprint as the guiding force in our lives, creating a life that reflects the infinite potential of the soul and the cosmos.

CHAPTER 16: THE ALCHEMY OF QUANTUM AND SPIRITUALITY

In the ancient laboratories of the alchemists, where fire and water danced in sacred union, where the elements of earth and air were transmuted into gold, there existed a belief—a belief that beneath the surface of material reality, a deeper, more profound transformation was possible. This transformation, known as alchemy, was not merely the transmutation of base metals into gold, but the elevation of the soul, the merging of the mundane with the divine. In the modern world, this ancient art finds a new expression at the intersection of quantum physics and spirituality—a dance of energies that has the potential to transform our understanding of the universe and our place within it. Inspired by Gary Zukav's The Dancing Wu Li Masters, this chapter explores the alchemy that occurs when quantum principles are integrated with spiritual wisdom, leading to profound shifts in consciousness and perception.

The Alchemy of Perception: Shifting from Separation to Unity

At the heart of both quantum physics and spirituality lies a fundamental shift in perception—a shift from seeing the world as a collection of separate, isolated objects to seeing it as an interconnected web of relationships, where everything is interdependent and connected. This shift is the first step in the alchemical process, a transformation that changes not just our understanding of the universe, but our experience of it.

In classical physics, the universe is seen as a vast machine, governed by deterministic laws that operate independently of human consciousness. This worldview, often referred to as the Newtonian paradigm, fosters a sense of separation—between the observer and the observed, between mind and matter, between self and other. It is a worldview that has shaped much of modern thought, influencing everything from science to philosophy, from economics to politics.

Quantum physics, however, offers a radically different perspective. It reveals a universe that is not a machine, but a dynamic, interconnected web of relationships, where the boundaries between observer and observed, mind and matter, self and other, begin to blur. In the quantum world, particles exist in a state of superposition, where they are not fixed in one location or state, but are spread out across a range of possibilities, until observed. This observer effect suggests that consciousness plays a crucial role in shaping reality, that the act of observation collapses the wave function, bringing one of these possibilities into actuality.

This shift from separation to unity is not just a change in perception; it is an alchemical transformation, one that opens the door to a deeper understanding of the universe and our place within it. It invites us to see the world not as a collection of separate parts, but as a unified whole, where everything is connected and interdependent. It challenges us to let go of the illusion of separateness, to recognize the interconnectedness of all things, and to embrace the unity that underlies the diversity of the universe.

The Alchemy of Mind and Matter: Transcending Duality

The integration of quantum physics and spirituality also involves the alchemical transformation of the relationship between mind and matter. In the classical worldview, mind and matter are seen as distinct and separate entities, with matter being the primary reality and mind being a secondary phenomenon that emerges from the physical brain. This dualistic view has led to a split between the spiritual and the material, between the inner world of thoughts and emotions and the outer world of physical objects and events.

Quantum physics, however, suggests that this duality is an illusion, that mind and matter are not separate, but are two aspects of the same underlying reality. The quantum field, which underlies all of physical reality, is not a material substance, but a field of potentialities, a realm of possibilities that exist in a state of superposition until observed. This suggests that consciousness is not a byproduct of the brain, but a fundamental aspect of reality, that mind and matter are deeply interconnected, and that the physical world is a manifestation of the deeper, non-material reality of the quantum field.

This understanding leads to a profound alchemical transformation, one that transcends the duality of mind and matter, and reveals the unity of all things. It invites us to see the physical world not as a separate, external reality, but as a reflection of our own consciousness, a manifestation of the deeper reality that underlies all of existence. It challenges us to transcend the illusion of duality, to recognize the unity of mind and matter, and to embrace the interconnectedness of all things.

The Alchemy of Time and Space: Beyond the Limits of the Material World

Another aspect of the alchemy that occurs at the intersection of quantum physics and spirituality is the transformation of our understanding of time and space. In the classical worldview, time and space are seen as fixed, absolute dimensions, within which all events occur. Time is linear, moving from past to present to future, and space is a three-dimensional arena, within which objects exist and move.

Quantum physics, however, reveals a different reality—one where time and space are not fixed and absolute, but are fluid and interconnected. In the quantum world, particles can be entangled, meaning that they can influence each other instantaneously, regardless of the distance between them, suggesting that space is not a barrier to their interaction. Similarly, the concept of superposition suggests that particles can exist in multiple states at once, challenging the linear nature of time.

This understanding leads to an alchemical transformation of our perception of time and space, revealing that they are not fixed dimensions, but are aspects of a deeper, more fluid reality. It invites us to see the world not as a rigid, deterministic system, but as a dynamic, evolving process, where the boundaries between past, present, and future, between here and there, begin to blur. It challenges us to let go of our attachment to the material world, to recognize the fluidity of time and space, and to embrace the infinite possibilities that exist within the quantum field.

The Alchemy of Consciousness: Awakening to the Quantum Self

The integration of quantum physics and spirituality also involves the alchemical transformation of consciousness, leading to the awakening of the quantum self. In the classical worldview, consciousness is seen as a product of the physical brain, a byproduct of chemical and electrical processes within the neurons. This view reduces consciousness to a mere epiphenomenon, a secondary effect of material processes, with no independent existence or significance.

Quantum physics, however, suggests that consciousness is not a byproduct of the brain, but a fundamental aspect of reality, one that plays a crucial role in shaping the physical world. The observer effect, which reveals that the act of observation collapses the wave function, suggests that consciousness is not passive, but active, that it plays a central role in the creation of reality. This understanding leads to the realization that we are not just physical beings, but quantum beings, with the power to shape our reality through our thoughts, intentions, and actions.

This realization leads to an alchemical transformation of consciousness, where we awaken to our true nature as quantum beings, connected to the deeper reality of the quantum field. It invites us to transcend the limitations of the material world, to recognize the power of consciousness to shape reality and embrace the infinite possibilities that exist within the quantum self. It challenges us to awaken to our true potential, to realize that we are not just passive observers of the world, but active participants in its creation, with the power to shape our destiny and the destiny of the universe.

The Alchemy of Transformation: Integrating Science and Spirituality

The alchemy that occurs at the intersection of quantum physics and spirituality is not just a theoretical concept; it is a practical process, one that has the power to transform our lives and our world. This transformation involves the integration of science and spirituality, the recognition that these two paths are not separate, but are complementary, each offering a unique perspective on the nature of reality.

This integration involves the recognition that science and spirituality are not in conflict, but are two sides of the same coin, each offering valuable insights into the nature of reality. Science offers a rigorous, empirical approach to understanding the physical world, revealing the underlying principles and laws that govern the universe. Spirituality offers a deeper, more intuitive approach, revealing the inner dimensions of reality, the interconnectedness of all things, and the sacredness of existence.

This integration leads to a profound transformation of our understanding of the universe and our place within it. It challenges us to let go of the rigid, deterministic worldview of classical physics, and to embrace the fluid, interconnected reality of the quantum world. It invites us to transcend the duality of mind and matter, to recognize the unity of all things, and to embrace the infinite possibilities that exist within the quantum field.

The Dance of the Alchemist: Embracing the Quantum Transformation

As we conclude this chapter, we are invited to embrace the alchemy that occurs at the intersection of quantum physics and spirituality, to recognize the profound transformation that is possible when these two paths are integrated. This transformation is not just about understanding the principles of quantum physics; it is about experiencing them, living them, and embodying them in every aspect of our lives.

The dance of the alchemist is a dance of integration, where science and spirituality come together in a harmonious union, revealing the deeper truths of the universe and our place within it. It is a dance that invites us to transcend the limitations of the material world, to awaken to our true nature as quantum beings, and to embrace the infinite possibilities that exist within the quantum field.

As we continue our journey into the heart of quantum

spirituality, let us carry this awareness with us, and let it guide us in the dance of life. Let us embrace the alchemy of quantum and spirituality, recognizing the profound transformation that is possible when these two paths are integrated, and let us create a life that reflects the beauty, harmony, and unity of the cosmos.

The alchemy of quantum and spirituality offers a profound transformation of our understanding of the universe and our place within it. By integrating the principles of quantum physics with the wisdom of spirituality, we can transcend the limitations of the material world, awaken to our true nature as quantum beings, and embrace the infinite possibilities that exist within the quantum field. As we explore the deeper truths of quantum spirituality, we are invited to embrace this alchemy as a path to transformation, creating a life that reflects the beauty, harmony, and unity of the cosmos.

CHAPTER 17: THE SACRED OBSERVER: THE POWER OF AWARENESS IN QUANTUM AND SPIRITUAL REALMS

In the vast, enigmatic theatre of the cosmos, where particles dance in the void and galaxies spiral through the infinity of space, there exists a presence —silent, watchful, and profoundly powerful. This presence is the observer, the sacred witness whose gaze holds the potential to bring forth reality from the realm of possibility. In both the quantum and spiritual realms, the observer plays a pivotal role, shaping the fabric of existence through the sheer act of awareness. Inspired by Nick Herbert's Quantum Reality, this chapter delves into the profound implications of the observer's role in quantum mechanics and spiritual practices, exploring how the power of awareness can be harnessed to live a more conscious, intentional, and spiritually attuned life.

The Quantum Observer: Shaping Reality Through Observation

At the heart of quantum mechanics lies a mystery that has puzzled and fascinated scientists and philosophers alike—the role of the observer in the creation of reality. Unlike the deterministic universe of classical physics, where events unfold according to fixed laws independent of observation, the quantum world reveals a different truth: the act of observation itself influences the outcome of events. This is the essence of the observer effect, a phenomenon that suggests that particles exist in a state of superposition—simultaneously in multiple states—until they are observed. It is the observer's gaze that collapses this superposition, bringing one possibility into reality.

This revelation challenges the traditional notion of an objective, external reality that exists independently of the observer. Instead, it suggests that reality is, at least in part, a construct of consciousness, a dynamic interplay between the observer and the observed. The observer effect implies that the universe is not a static, predetermined entity, but a fluid, malleable process that responds to the presence of awareness.

In the quantum realm, the observer is not merely a passive spectator; they are an active participant in the creation of reality. This understanding opens the door to a profound realization: that our thoughts, perceptions, and intentions play a crucial role in shaping the world around us. The observer effect invites us to consider the possibility that we are not merely inhabitants of the universe, but co-creators, weaving the fabric of reality through the power of our awareness.

The Sacred Observer: Awareness in Spiritual Practice

The role of the observer is not confined to the realm of quantum mechanics; it is a central theme in many spiritual traditions, where awareness is seen as the key to unlocking the mysteries of existence. In these traditions, the observer is often referred to as the witness—the silent, unchanging presence that observes the flow of thoughts, emotions, and experiences without becoming entangled in them. This witness is the essence of consciousness, the true self that lies beyond the fluctuations of the mind and the impermanence of the material world.

In spiritual practices such as meditation, mindfulness, and contemplation, the cultivation of awareness is seen as a path to enlightenment, a means of transcending the limitations of the ego and accessing the deeper truths of existence. By developing the ability to observe our thoughts, emotions, and sensations with detachment and clarity, we begin to see through the illusions of the mind and recognize the underlying unity of all things. This shift in awareness is often described as a spiritual awakening—a realization of our true nature as consciousness itself, beyond the confines of the individual self.

The concept of the sacred observer invites us to explore the connection between quantum mechanics and spiritual practice, to recognize that the power of observation is not limited to the physical realm but extends into the spiritual dimensions of existence. Just as the quantum observer shapes reality through the act of observation, so too does the sacred observer shape our inner and outer worlds through the power of awareness. This awareness is not just a passive state of being; it is an active, creative force that has the potential to transform our lives and our understanding of the universe.

The Alchemy of Awareness: Transforming Reality Through Conscious Observation

The integration of quantum mechanics and spirituality reveals a profound truth: that awareness is a powerful tool for transformation, a means by which we can shape our reality and align ourselves with the deeper currents of the cosmos. This alchemy of awareness involves recognizing the impact of our thoughts, beliefs, and intentions on the world around us, and using this understanding to live more consciously and intentionally.

In the quantum realm, the observer effect demonstrates that the act of observation collapses the wave function, bringing potentialities into actuality. This suggests that by directing our awareness towards certain possibilities, we can influence the outcome of events, bringing our intentions into manifestation. This process is not limited to the quantum level; it extends into every aspect of our lives, where our thoughts and beliefs shape our experiences and interactions with the world.

The practice of conscious observation involves cultivating a state of mindfulness, where we become aware of the thoughts and emotions that arise within us and recognize their influence on our reality. By observing our inner landscape with clarity and detachment, we can begin to identify the patterns and beliefs that shape our experiences and make conscious choices that align with our highest aspirations. This practice is not about controlling or manipulating reality; it is about aligning ourselves with the deeper truths of existence and allowing the natural flow of the universe to guide our actions and decisions.

In spiritual terms, the alchemy of awareness involves recognizing the sacredness of the present moment and using our awareness to connect with the divine presence that permeates all of existence. This connection is not something that can be forced or fabricated; it arises naturally when we cultivate a state of open, receptive awareness, where we are fully present to the mystery and beauty of life. In this state, we become attuned to the subtle energies and vibrations of the universe, and our actions become an expression of the divine will.

The Power of Presence: Living in Alignment with the Quantum and Spiritual Realms

The role of the observer in both quantum mechanics and spirituality points to a deeper truth: the power of awareness lies in our ability to be fully present in the moment, to engage with reality as it unfolds, and to shape our experience through conscious observation. This power of presence is the key to living in alignment with the quantum and spiritual realms, where the boundaries between the physical and the metaphysical dissolve, and the sacred becomes a tangible reality.

Living in alignment with the quantum and spiritual realms involves cultivating a state of presence where we are fully aware of our thoughts, emotions, and surroundings, and where we engage with the world from a place of deep connection and inner stillness. This state of presence is not about withdrawing from the world or escaping into a meditative trance; it is about bringing the qualities of mindfulness, awareness, and intention into every aspect of our lives.

In practical terms, this means developing the habit of pausing throughout the day to check in with us, to observe our thoughts and feelings, and to make conscious choices that reflect our highest values and aspirations. It means practicing mindfulness in our interactions with others, listening deeply and responding with compassion and empathy. It means approaching our work and daily activities with a sense of purpose and intention, recognizing that every action has the potential to influence the quantum field and contribute to the unfolding of reality.

The power of presence also involves recognizing the interconnectedness of all things and living in a way that reflects this awareness. This means cultivating a sense of reverence for the natural world, recognizing that we are not separate from the earth, but are part of a larger, interconnected web of life. It means embracing the principle of non-harm, where we strive to live in a way that minimizes our impact on the environment and promotes the well-being of all beings.

The Journey of the Sacred Observer: Awakening to the Power of Awareness

As we conclude this chapter, we are invited to embrace the journey of the sacred observer, to recognize the power of awareness in shaping our reality, and to live more consciously and intentionally in both the quantum and spiritual realms. This journey is not about attaining a state of perfect enlightenment or mastering the mysteries of the universe; it is about awakening to the truth of who we are and learning to live in harmony with the deeper currents of existence.

The journey of the sacred observer is a path of self-discovery, where we explore the depths of our consciousness and the nature of reality, and where we cultivate the qualities of mindfulness, presence, and intention. It is a journey that requires us to let go of old patterns and beliefs, and to embrace the infinite possibilities that exist within the quantum field. It is a journey that challenges us to live with greater awareness, to recognize the impact of our thoughts and actions on the world, and to align ourselves with the divine will.

As we continue our journey into the heart of quantum spirituality, let us carry this awareness with us, and let it guide us in the dance of life. Let us embrace the power of the sacred observer, recognizing the profound impact of our awareness on reality, and let us use this power to create a life that reflects the beauty, harmony, and unity of the cosmos.

The sacred observer, as revealed in both quantum mechanics and spiritual practice, offers a profound understanding of the power of awareness in shaping reality. By embracing the role of the observer, we can live more consciously and intentionally, aligning ourselves with the deeper truths of existence and the divine will. As we explore the deeper dimensions of quantum spirituality, we are invited to harness the power of awareness to create a life that reflects the infinite potential of the quantum field and the sacredness of the spiritual realm.

CHAPTER 18: THE QUANTUM KEY: UNLOCKING THE SECRETS OF THE UNIVERSE AND THE SOUL

In the silent spaces between the ticking of time, in the luminous depths of the cosmos where light and shadow dance in eternal interplay, there lies a key—a key not forged from metal, but from the very fabric of existence. This is the quantum key, a metaphorical yet profoundly real tool that holds the potential to unlock the deepest mysteries of the universe and the most sacred secrets of the soul. Inspired by Quantum God by Ted Peters and Martinez Hewlett, this chapter explores the idea of the quantum key as a means of accessing the hidden knowledge that bridges the scientific and spiritual realms. Through the integration of these two paths, we embark on a journey to unlock the door to a more complete understanding of our existence.

The Quest for the Quantum Key: The Interplay of Science and Spirituality

The quest for understanding the universe has been the driving force behind both scientific inquiry and spiritual exploration for millennia. Science, with its empirical methods and logical frameworks, seeks to decode the mechanics of the cosmos—the "how" of existence. Spirituality, with its emphasis on inner experience and transcendence, seeks to uncover the meaning and purpose behind the cosmos—the "why" of existence. These two approaches have often been seen as separate, even conflicting paths, but the concept of the quantum key suggests that they are in fact complementary, each offering a vital piece of the puzzle that is our reality.

The quantum key represents the convergence of these two paths, a symbolic tool that can unlock the secrets of both the universe and the soul. It is a metaphor for the knowledge and wisdom that arise when scientific understanding is integrated with spiritual insight, revealing a more holistic and unified view of reality. This key is not something that can be found in a textbook or a scripture; it is something that must be forged through the synthesis of knowledge, experience, and intuition—a process that requires both the rigor of science and the depth of spirituality.

In the quantum world, the universe is not a static, mechanistic system, but a dynamic, interconnected web of relationships, where the observer plays an active role in the creation of reality. This understanding challenges the traditional boundaries between science and spirituality, suggesting that the mysteries of the universe and the soul are not separate, but are intertwined in a complex dance of energy and consciousness. The quantum key is the tool that allows us to access this deeper understanding, to unlock the doors that separate the material from the spiritual, and to discover the unity that lies at the heart of existence.

The Structure of the Quantum Key: Integrating Knowledge and Wisdom

To forge the quantum key, we must first understand its structure—how scientific knowledge and spiritual wisdom come together to create a tool that can unlock the secrets of the universe and the soul. This structure is not rigid or fixed; it is fluid and dynamic, reflecting the ever-evolving nature of both science and spirituality. It is composed of several interlocking elements, each of which contributes to the key's ability to open the doors of understanding.

The Element of Empirical Knowledge: At the core of the quantum key lies the element of empirical knowledge —the understanding of the physical world that comes from observation, experimentation, and analysis. This element represents the scientific approach to knowledge, where theories are tested and refined through rigorous methods, and where the laws of nature are uncovered through careful study. Empirical knowledge is essential for understanding the mechanics of the universe, from the behaviour of subatomic particles to the evolution of galaxies. It provides the foundation upon which our understanding of the physical world is built, offering insights into the "how" of existence.

The Element of Intuitive Wisdom: Complementing empirical knowledge is the element of intuitive wisdom—the understanding that arises from inner experience, reflection, and spiritual practice. This element represents the spiritual approach to knowledge, where truths are discovered through meditation, contemplation, and connection with the divine. Intuitive wisdom is essential for understanding the meaning and purpose of existence, offering insights into the "why" of life. It provides the depth and richness that empirical knowledge alone cannot offer, revealing the underlying patterns and principles that govern the universe and the soul.

The Element of Synthesis: The final element of the quantum key is synthesis—the process of bringing together empirical knowledge and intuitive wisdom to create a more complete and holistic understanding of reality. Synthesis is not about forcing these two approaches into a single framework, but about recognizing their complementary nature and allowing them to inform and enrich each other. This element is what gives the quantum key its power, enabling it to unlock the doors that separate the material from the spiritual, the scientific from the mystical. Through synthesis, we discover that the universe and the soul are not separate entities but are reflections of the same underlying reality.

Unlocking the Secrets of the Universe: The Role of the Quantum Key in Science

The quantum key offers a new way of understanding

the universe, one that goes beyond the limitations of classical physics and embraces the complexity and interconnectedness of the quantum world. In the realm of quantum mechanics, the universe is not a deterministic machine, but a dynamic, evolving process, where particles exist in a state of potential until they are observed, and where the observer plays a crucial role in shaping reality. This understanding challenges the traditional boundaries of science, opening the door to a more holistic and integrated view of the cosmos.

With the quantum key, we can unlock the secrets of the universe by recognizing the role of consciousness in the creation of reality. This involves understanding that the laws of nature are not fixed and immutable, but are influenced by the observer's consciousness, and that the physical world is not separate from the spiritual but is a manifestation of the underlying quantum field. By integrating scientific knowledge with spiritual wisdom, we can develop a more complete understanding of the universe, one that acknowledges the role of consciousness and the interconnectedness of all things.

The quantum key also allows us to explore the deeper dimensions of reality, beyond the limitations of time and space. In the quantum world, particles can be entangled, meaning that they can influence each other instantaneously, regardless of the distance between them. This phenomenon challenges our traditional understanding of causality and suggests that the universe is a unified whole, where everything is interconnected and interdependent. With the quantum key, we can explore these deeper dimensions, uncovering the hidden patterns and principles that govern the cosmos and discovering the unity that lies at the heart of existence.

Unlocking the Secrets of the Soul: The Role of the Quantum Key in Spirituality

Just as the quantum key can unlock the secrets of the universe, it can also unlock the secrets of the soul, offering a deeper understanding of our true nature and our place in the cosmos. In the realm of spirituality, the quantum key reveals that the soul is not a separate, isolated entity, but is deeply connected to the quantum field—the underlying fabric of reality. This understanding challenges the traditional boundaries of spirituality, opening the door to a more integrated and holistic view of the self.

With the quantum key, we can explore the deeper dimensions of the soul by recognizing the role of consciousness in shaping our inner reality. This involves understanding that our thoughts, emotions, and intentions are not separate from the quantum field, but are expressions of it, and that our inner world is not separate from the outer world but is deeply interconnected with it. By integrating spiritual wisdom with scientific knowledge, we can develop a more complete understanding of the soul, one that acknowledges the role of consciousness and the interconnectedness of all things.

The quantum key also allows us to explore the deeper dimensions of the soul, beyond the limitations of the ego and the material world. In the quantum world, consciousness is not confined to the brain, but is a field of potential, where the boundaries between self and other, mind and matter, begin to blur. This understanding challenges our traditional understanding of the self and invites us to explore the deeper dimensions of our being, where the soul is not a fixed and separate entity, but a dynamic and evolving process, deeply connected to the quantum field.

The Alchemy of Knowledge: Forging the Quantum Key

Forging the quantum key requires the integration of scientific knowledge and spiritual wisdom, creating a tool that can unlock the secrets of both the universe and the soul. This alchemical process involves the recognition that science and spirituality are not separate or conflicting paths but are complementary approaches to understanding reality. By bringing these two paths together, we can create a more complete and holistic understanding of existence, one that acknowledges the role of consciousness, the interconnectedness of all things, and the unity that lies at the heart of the cosmos.

The alchemy of knowledge involves several key practices that help to forge the quantum key:

Contemplative Science: This practice involves approaching scientific inquiry with a sense of reverence and wonder, recognizing that the study of the natural world is not just an intellectual pursuit, but a spiritual practice. Contemplative science involves exploring the mysteries of the universe with an open mind and an open heart, allowing scientific knowledge to inform and enrich our spiritual understanding.

Integrative Meditation: This practice involves combining meditation with scientific exploration, using the mind as a tool for exploring both the inner and outer dimensions of reality. Integrative meditation involves contemplating the principles of quantum physics in light of spiritual teachings, allowing these insights to deepen our understanding of both the universe and the soul.

Holistic Learning: This practice involves integrating knowledge from multiple disciplines, recognizing that no single field of study can provide a complete understanding of reality. Holistic learning involves exploring the connections between science, spirituality, philosophy, and other fields, creating a more integrated and holistic understanding of existence.

Embodied Wisdom: This practice involves applying the insights gained from the quantum key to our daily lives, living in a way that reflects our understanding of the interconnectedness of all things. Embodied wisdom involves aligning our thoughts, actions, and intentions with the deeper truths of existence, creating a life that reflects the unity and harmony of the cosmos.

The Journey of Discovery: Using the Quantum Key to Unlock the Secrets of Existence

As we conclude this chapter, we are invited to embark on a journey of discovery, using the quantum key to unlock the secrets of the universe and the soul. This journey is not about accumulating knowledge for its own sake, but about deepening our understanding of existence and our place within it. It is a journey that challenges us to integrate scientific knowledge with spiritual wisdom, creating a more complete and holistic understanding of reality.

The journey of discovery involves exploring the mysteries of the universe with an open mind and an open heart, recognizing that the quantum key is not a fixed or static tool, but a dynamic and evolving process. It involves cultivating a sense of wonder and reverence for the natural world, recognizing that science and spirituality are not separate paths, but are complementary approaches to understanding existence.

As we continue our journey into the heart of quantum spirituality, let us carry the quantum key with us, using it to unlock the doors that separate the material from the spiritual, the scientific from the mystical. Let us embrace the alchemy of knowledge, recognizing the power of the quantum key to reveal the unity and harmony that lie at the heart of existence, and let us use this understanding to create a life that reflects the beauty, wisdom, and interconnectedness of the cosmos.

The quantum key offers a profound tool for unlocking the secrets of both the universe and the soul. By integrating scientific knowledge with spiritual wisdom, we can create a more complete and holistic understanding of existence, one that acknowledges the role of consciousness and the interconnectedness of all things. As we explore the deeper dimensions of quantum spirituality, we are invited to use the quantum key to unlock the doors that separate the material from the spiritual, and to discover the unity that lies at the heart of the cosmos.

CHAPTER 19: THE SACRED WAVE: RIDING THE QUANTUM CURRENTS OF LIFE

In the silent stillness of the universe, where the infinitesimal meets the infinite, there exists a rhythm—a pulse that beats in time with the heart of existence itself. This rhythm is carried by the quantum wave, a sacred current that flows through the very fabric of reality, guiding the dance of particles, stars, and souls alike. Inspired by Quantum Questions, edited by Ken Wilber, this chapter delves into the concept of the quantum wave as a divine current that permeates all of life. It invites us to learn how to ride these sacred waves, aligning our lives with the deeper rhythms of the universe, and in doing so, to find our place within the grand cosmic symphony.

The Quantum Wave: The Sacred Pulse of Existence

At the heart of quantum physics lies the concept of the wave function—a mathematical description of the probabilities associated with the position, momentum, and other properties of a quantum system. This wave function is not merely a static equation; it is a dynamic, living entity, representing the potentialities that exist before they are observed and collapsed into a single reality. The quantum wave is the manifestation of this function in motion—a sacred pulse that flows through all matter and energy, connecting everything in a web of possibility.

In many ways, the quantum wave can be seen as the heartbeat of the universe, a rhythm that underlies all of existence. It is a pattern that repeats itself at every level of reality, from the smallest particles to the largest galaxies, creating a sense of order and harmony amidst the apparent chaos. This wave is not confined to the physical realm; it extends into the metaphysical, resonating with the spiritual dimensions of existence and guiding the evolution of consciousness.

To perceive the quantum wave is to glimpse the sacred order of the cosmos, to recognize that life is not a series of random events, but a deeply interconnected and purposeful process. The wave function's undulations reflect the flow of time, the cycle of creation and destruction, the ebb and flow of energy and matter. It is a reminder that everything in the universe is in motion, constantly evolving and transforming, yet bound together by a common rhythm—a rhythm that we can learn to attune ourselves to, if we listen closely enough.

Riding the Quantum Currents: Aligning with the Rhythms of the Universe

To ride the quantum currents of life is to align oneself with the deeper rhythms of the universe, to move in harmony with the sacred wave rather than against it. This alignment is not something that can be forced or manufactured; it is a process of attunement, of learning to listen to the subtle cues that the universe offers and responding to them with grace and fluidity.

In practical terms, riding the quantum currents involves cultivating a state of presence and awareness, where we become attuned to the ebb and flow of energy in our lives and learn to move in sync with it. This requires us to let go of rigid expectations and control, and to embrace a more flexible and responsive way of being, one that is open to the unexpected and the unknown.

Mindfulness is one of the key practices that can help us attune to the quantum currents. By cultivating a state of mindful awareness, we can become more attuned to the present moment, sensing the subtle shifts in energy and responding to them with intention and clarity. Mindfulness allows us to observe the flow of thoughts, emotions, and sensations within us, and to recognize how these inner currents are connected to the larger currents of the universe. By riding these inner waves with awareness, we can align ourselves with the deeper rhythms of life, moving in harmony with the sacred wave.

Meditation is another powerful tool for attuning to the quantum currents. In meditation, we quiet the mind and open the heart, creating a space where we can listen to the subtle vibrations of the quantum wave and feel its presence within us. Through meditation, we can connect with the deeper layers of our consciousness, where the sacred wave is most palpable, and learn to ride its currents with grace and ease. This practice helps us cultivate a sense of inner stillness and peace, even amidst the turbulence of life, allowing us to navigate the ups and downs of existence with equanimity and balance.

Intuition is also an essential aspect of riding the quantum currents. Intuition is the inner knowing that arises when we are in tune with the deeper rhythms of the universe, a sense of guidance that helps us navigate the complexities of life. By listening to our intuition, we can tap into the wisdom of the quantum wave, allowing it to guide our decisions and actions in ways that align with our highest purpose. Intuition is not something that can be forced or manufactured; it is a natural response to being in harmony with the sacred wave, a resonance that arises when we are attuned to the deeper truths of existence.

The Sacred Dance: Moving in Harmony with the Quantum Wave

Riding the quantum currents is not just about navigating the challenges of life; it is about participating in the sacred dance of existence, moving in harmony with the rhythms of the universe. This dance is not a solitary endeavour; it is a collective experience, where all beings are connected by the same sacred wave, moving together in a grand cosmic symphony.

In this dance, we are not passive participants, but active co-creators, shaping the flow of energy and matter through our thoughts, intentions, and actions. The quantum wave responds to our presence, reflecting our consciousness and influencing the unfolding of reality. By moving in harmony with the wave, we can create a life that reflects the beauty, harmony, and unity of the cosmos, a life that is in sync with the deeper rhythms of existence.

The sacred dance is also a reminder that life is not static or fixed, but is constantly in motion, evolving and transforming in response to the flow of the quantum wave. This understanding challenges us to embrace change and uncertainty, recognizing that the currents of life are always shifting, and that our ability to ride these currents with grace and fluidity is the key to navigating the complexities of existence.

The Alchemy of Surrender: Letting Go and Trusting the Wave

One of the most profound lessons of the quantum wave is the importance of surrender—of letting go of control and trusting in the flow of the universe. The sacred wave is a powerful force, one that is beyond our ability to manipulate or direct. It is a reminder that life is not something that can be controlled or predicted but is a dynamic and ever-changing process, guided by forces that are greater than ourselves.

Surrendering to the quantum wave does not mean giving up or resigning ourselves to fate; it means embracing the flow of life with openness and trust, recognizing that the universe is always moving in the direction of growth and evolution. It means letting go of our attachment to outcomes and allowing the wave to carry us where we need to go, trusting that the currents of life will guide us to the experiences and opportunities that are most aligned with our highest purpose.

The alchemy of surrender is a transformative process, one that requires us to release our fears and doubts and to embrace the unknown with courage and faith. It is a process of learning to trust in the wisdom of the universe, recognizing that the quantum wave is always moving in the direction of balance and harmony and that by aligning ourselves with this flow, we can navigate the challenges of life with grace and ease.

The Journey of the Sacred Wave: Embracing the Flow of Life

As we conclude this chapter, we are invited to embrace the journey of the sacred wave, to learn how to ride the quantum currents of life with awareness, grace, and trust. This journey is not about mastering the wave or controlling its flow; it is about becoming attuned to its presence within us and around us and learning to move in harmony with its rhythms.

The journey of the sacred wave is a path of self-discovery, where we learn to navigate the complexities of existence with mindfulness, intuition, and surrender. It is a journey that challenges us to let go of our attachment to control and to embrace the flow of life with openness and trust. It is a journey that invites us to participate in the sacred dance of existence, to become co-creators in the grand cosmic symphony, and to live a life that reflects the beauty, harmony, and unity of the cosmos.

As we continue our journey into the heart of quantum spirituality, let us carry the wisdom of the sacred wave with us, using it to guide our actions, decisions, and relationships. Let us embrace the quantum currents of life, recognizing the sacredness of the wave and the power it holds to transform our understanding of the universe and our place within it. And let us trust in the flow of the universe, knowing that by aligning ourselves with the deeper rhythms of existence, we can navigate the challenges of life with grace, fluidity, and wisdom.

The sacred wave, as revealed through the quantum currents of life, offers a profound understanding of the rhythms and patterns that underlie existence. By learning to ride these currents, we can align our lives with the deeper rhythms of the universe, creating a life that reflects the beauty, harmony, and unity of the cosmos. As we explore the deeper dimensions of quantum spirituality, we are invited to embrace the sacred wave as a guiding force in our lives, and to trust in the flow of the universe as we navigate the complexities of existence.

CHAPTER 20: THE QUANTUM AWAKENING: A CALL TO SPIRITUAL CONSCIOUSNESS

In the silent, pulsating heart of the universe, where the invisible threads of reality weave together the fabric of existence, there lies a truth—a truth so profound that it beckons us to awaken from the slumber of separation and step into the light of unity. This is the quantum awakening, a call to recognize the interconnectedness of all minds, a call to rise into a new level of spiritual consciousness where the boundaries between self and other dissolve, revealing the oneness of all existence. Inspired by Dean Radin's Entangled Minds, this chapter serves as both an invitation and a challenge: an invitation to explore the spiritual implications of quantum physics, and a challenge to embrace the awareness of our interconnectedness as a pathway to a global spiritual awakening.

The Web of Consciousness: Interconnected Minds in the Quantum Field

At the core of quantum physics lies a phenomenon that defies conventional logic—a phenomenon known as quantum entanglement. When particles become entangled, their states become linked, such that the state of one particle instantly influences the state of another, regardless of the distance separating them. This "spooky action at a distance," as Einstein famously described it, suggests that the universe is far more interconnected than we might have ever imagined.

But entanglement is not confined to the realm of subatomic particles. As Dean Radin explores in Entangled Minds, there is compelling evidence to suggest that this quantum phenomenon extends to the realm of consciousness as well. Our minds, it seems, are not isolated islands of awareness, but are intricately connected through an invisible web of consciousness, a field that transcends the physical boundaries of space and time.

This interconnectedness implies that our thoughts, emotions, and intentions are not confined to our individual minds, but ripple outwards, influencing the collective consciousness in ways we are only beginning to understand. It suggests that we are all part of a larger, interconnected whole, a vast network of minds that are entangled at the deepest levels of reality. This realization challenges the traditional notion of the self as a separate, isolated entity and invites us to see ourselves as integral parts of a greater, interconnected consciousness.

The Spiritual Implications of Quantum Interconnectedness

The recognition of our interconnectedness through quantum entanglement has profound spiritual implications. It suggests that the boundaries we perceive between self and other, between mind and matter, are illusory—constructs of our limited perception that obscure the deeper truth of our unity. This understanding invites us to expand our sense of self, to see our consciousness not as a separate entity, but as a thread in the vast tapestry of universal consciousness.

This expanded sense of self is not merely an intellectual concept; it is a lived experience, one that can transform our understanding of reality and our relationship to the world around us. When we recognize that our thoughts and intentions are entangled with those of others, we begin to understand the power of our consciousness to influence the collective field. This awareness challenges us to take responsibility for the energy we bring into the world, to recognize that our inner states of being —our thoughts, emotions, and intentions—have a direct impact on the collective consciousness.

The spiritual implications of quantum interconnectedness also extend to the way we relate to others. When we understand that we are all connected at the deepest levels of reality, we begin to see others not as separate beings, but as reflections of ourselves. This recognition fosters a sense of compassion, empathy, and unity, dissolving the barriers of judgment and separation that divide us. It encourages us to act from a place of love and kindness, recognizing that what we do to others, we do to ourselves.

The Call to Awakening: Embracing the Quantum Consciousness

The quantum awakening is a call to embrace this expanded awareness of our interconnectedness, to recognize the profound implications of quantum physics for our spiritual lives, and to rise into a new level of consciousness. This awakening is not just an individual process; it is a collective one, a global shift in consciousness that has the potential to transform the way we live, relate, and coexist on this planet.

To answer this call to awakening, we must first cultivate the awareness of our interconnectedness. This involves developing a deeper understanding of the quantum nature of reality, exploring the ways in which our consciousness is entangled with that of others, and recognizing the power we have to influence the collective field. It also involves cultivating practices that help us attune to this interconnectedness, such as meditation, mindfulness, and intentional living.

Meditation is one of the most powerful tools for cultivating quantum consciousness. Through meditation, we can quiet the mind, open the heart, and connect with the deeper layers of our consciousness, where the threads of interconnectedness are most palpable. Meditation allows us to transcend the boundaries of the ego, to experience the unity of all things, and to align our intentions with the higher frequencies of love, compassion, and unity.

Mindfulness is another essential practice for embracing quantum consciousness. By cultivating mindfulness in our daily lives, we can become more aware of the subtle energies that flow through us and around us and learn to navigate the complexities of existence with greater clarity and intention. Mindfulness helps us to stay connected to the present moment, where the sacredness of interconnectedness can be felt and experienced.

Intentional living involves aligning our thoughts, emotions, and actions with the awareness of our interconnectedness. It means recognizing that every choice we make, every word we speak, and every action we take, has an impact on the collective consciousness. By living with intention, we can contribute to the creation of a more harmonious, compassionate, and spiritually awakened world.

The Global Spiritual Awakening: A Vision for the Future

The quantum awakening is not just a personal journey; it is a vision for the future, a call to action for humanity to rise to a new level of collective consciousness. This global spiritual awakening is the next step in our evolution, a shift that has the potential to transform our world from one of division and conflict to one of unity and cooperation.

This vision for the future is not a utopian dream; it is a possibility that is already unfolding, as more and more people awaken to the reality of our interconnectedness and begin to live in alignment with this awareness. The quantum awakening is a ripple effect, where the awakening of one individual consciousness has the potential to influence the collective field, inspiring others to awaken and contributing to the creation of a critical mass of awakened beings.

The global spiritual awakening involves the integration of science and spirituality, where the insights of quantum physics are embraced not just as scientific theories, but as spiritual truths that have the power to transform our understanding of reality. It involves the recognition that the boundaries between science and spirituality, between self and other, between mind and matter, are dissolving, revealing the unity that lies at the heart of existence.

This awakening also involves a shift in our values, where love, compassion, and unity become the guiding principles of our lives, and where the well-being of all beings is recognized as interconnected with our own. It challenges us to live in a way that reflects our awareness of interconnectedness, to act from a place of kindness and empathy, and to contribute to the creation of a more just, peaceful, and spiritually awakened world.

Answering the Call: Embracing the Quantum Awakening

As we conclude this chapter, we are invited to answer the call to quantum awakening, to embrace the spiritual implications of quantum physics, and to rise to a new level of consciousness. This awakening is not just a personal journey; it is a collective one, a global shift in consciousness that has the potential to transform our world.

Answering the call to quantum awakening involves cultivating the awareness of our interconnectedness, recognizing the power of our consciousness to influence the collective field, and living in a way that reflects this awareness. It challenges us to let go of the illusion of separation, to embrace the reality of unity, and to act from a place of love, compassion, and unity.

As we continue our journey into the heart of quantum spirituality, let us carry this awareness with us, using it to guide our thoughts, actions, and relationships. Let us embrace the quantum awakening as a pathway to a more spiritually awakened world and let us contribute to the creation of a global consciousness that reflects the beauty, harmony, and unity of the cosmos.

The quantum awakening is a call to recognize the interconnectedness of all minds and to rise into a new level of spiritual consciousness. By embracing the spiritual implications of quantum physics, we can contribute to a global spiritual awakening, creating a world that reflects the unity and harmony of the cosmos. As we explore the deeper dimensions of quantum spirituality, we are invited to answer the call to quantum awakening, living in alignment with the awareness of our interconnectedness and contributing to the creation of a more spiritually awakened world.

CHAPTER 21: THE QUANTUM RITUALS: SACRED PRACTICES FOR MODERN TIMES

In the intersection of the ancient and the modern, where the timeless wisdom of spirituality meets the cutting-edge revelations of quantum physics, there lies a new path—a path that honours both the scientific and the sacred, weaving them together into a harmonious way of life. This path is embodied in what we might call quantum rituals—sacred practices designed for modern times that integrate the principles of quantum mechanics with the deep, transformative power of spiritual traditions. Inspired by The Quantum Enigma by Bruce Rosenblum and Fred Kuttner, this chapter offers practical guidance on how to incorporate these quantum rituals into our daily lives, helping us to live in a way that honours both the material and the mystical, the empirical and the ineffable.

The Essence of Quantum Rituals: Bridging Science and Spirituality

At the heart of quantum rituals is the recognition that reality is not a fixed, static construct, but a dynamic, ever-evolving interplay of consciousness, energy, and matter. Quantum physics reveals a universe that is deeply interconnected, where the act of observation influences the outcome of events, and where the boundaries between the observer and the observed, mind and matter, begin to blur. This understanding challenges us to rethink the way we engage with the world, inviting us to live with greater awareness of the subtle forces that shape our reality.

Quantum rituals are practices that bridge the gap between science and spirituality, offering a way to honour the mysteries of the quantum world while grounding ourselves in the sacred traditions that have guided humanity for millennia. These rituals are not about replacing ancient practices with modern science, but about integrating the insights of quantum physics into our spiritual lives, creating a holistic approach to living that honours both the seen and the unseen, the measurable and the mystical.

Daily Quantum Practices: Integrating Awareness into Everyday Life

The foundation of quantum rituals is the practice of bringing awareness into every aspect of our daily lives.

This awareness is not just a mental exercise; it is a way of being, a way of attuning ourselves to the deeper currents of reality and aligning our actions, thoughts, and intentions with the principles of quantum interconnectedness and unity.

Mindful Observation: One of the simplest yet most profound quantum practices is mindful observation. This practice involves cultivating a state of presence and awareness in everything we do, from the mundane tasks of daily life to the most significant moments of decision and reflection. By observing our thoughts, emotions, and actions with mindfulness, we become more attuned to the subtle energies that flow through us and around us, recognizing how our consciousness influences the reality we experience. Mindful observation is a way of aligning ourselves with the quantum principle that the act of observation shapes reality, reminding us that our awareness is a powerful tool for creating the life we wish to live.

Intention Setting: Another key practice in quantum rituals is the setting of intentions. In the quantum world, the observer plays a crucial role in collapsing the wave function, bringing potentialities into actuality. Similarly, in our spiritual lives, the intentions we set shape the outcomes we experience. By setting clear, conscious intentions each day, we align ourselves with the quantum field, directing our energy and focus towards the realization of our goals and aspirations. This practice is not just about achieving external success; it is about aligning our inner world with our highest values and deepest truths, creating a life that reflects the harmony and balance of the cosmos.

Quantum Meditation: Meditation has long been a cornerstone of spiritual practice, and when integrated with quantum principles, it becomes a powerful tool for aligning ourselves with the deeper rhythms of the universe. Quantum meditation involves entering a state of deep relaxation and openness, where we can connect with the quantum field—the underlying fabric of reality that connects all things. In this state, we can visualize ourselves as part of the interconnected web of existence, allowing the flow of energy and consciousness to guide us towards greater clarity, insight, and alignment. Quantum meditation helps us to transcend the limitations of the ego and to experience the unity of all things, fostering a sense of peace and oneness with the universe.

Gratitude and Resonance: Gratitude is a powerful practice that aligns us with the higher frequencies of love and abundance. In the context of quantum spirituality, gratitude is more than just a positive emotion; it is a way of resonating with the quantum field, amplifying the energy of what we are grateful for and attracting more of it into our lives. By cultivating a daily practice of gratitude, we tune our consciousness to the vibrations of abundance, aligning ourselves with the flow of life and the benevolent forces of the universe. This practice can be as simple as taking a few moments each day to reflect on the things we are grateful for, or as elaborate as creating a gratitude journal where we record our blessings and insights.

Sacred Rituals of Connection: Quantum rituals also include practices that deepen our connection with the world around us, reminding us of our interconnectedness with all life. These rituals can take many forms, from spending time in nature and appreciating the beauty of the natural world, to participating in community activities that foster a sense of unity and shared purpose. By engaging in rituals that celebrate our connection to the earth, to other beings, and to the cosmos, we reinforce the awareness that we are not separate from the world but are an integral part of the great web of existence. These rituals help us to cultivate a sense of reverence and respect for all life, aligning our actions with the principle of non-harm and the pursuit of the greater good.

Rituals for Modern Times: Adapting Ancient Wisdom to Contemporary Life

One of the challenges of living in the modern world is finding ways to integrate ancient spiritual wisdom into our fast-paced, technologically driven lives. Quantum rituals offer a way to adapt these timeless teachings to the realities of contemporary life, creating practices that are both meaningful and relevant to our current circumstances.

Digital Detox and Quantum Reflection: In a world that is increasingly dominated by digital technology, one of the most powerful rituals we can adopt is the practice of digital detox—a period of time where we disconnect from our devices and reconnect with ourselves, our loved ones, and the natural world. During this time, we can engage in quantum reflection, a practice of introspection and meditation where we contemplate the deeper questions of existence and align ourselves with the quantum principles of interconnectedness and unity. This practice helps us to break free from the constant barrage of information and stimuli that can overwhelm our senses, allowing us to tune into the more subtle energies of the quantum field and gain clarity on our path.

Rituals of Silence and Stillness: In a culture that values productivity and constant activity, the practice of silence and stillness can be a radical act of spiritual alignment. By creating space for silence and stillness in our daily lives, we can cultivate a deeper connection with the quantum field and the inner wisdom that arises from it. These rituals can take the form of morning or evening meditations, silent walks in nature, or moments of quiet reflection throughout the day. By embracing silence and stillness, we allow ourselves to attune to the deeper rhythms of the universe, fostering a sense of inner peace and balance that carries over into all aspects of our lives.

Rituals of Creativity and Expression: Creativity is a powerful way to connect with the quantum field, as it allows us to channel the infinite potentialities of the universe into tangible form. Rituals of creativity and expression can include activities such as painting, writing, dancing, or playing music—any form of creative expression that resonates with our soul. By engaging in these rituals, we tap into the flow of the quantum wave, allowing it to guide our creative process and bring forth new insights, ideas, and manifestations. These rituals remind us that we are co-creators with the universe, capable of bringing our visions and dreams into reality through the power of intention and expression.

Living the Quantum Spirituality: A Holistic Approach to Life

The ultimate goal of quantum rituals is to create a holistic approach to life—one that honours both the scientific and the sacred, the material and the mystical. By integrating these practices into our daily lives, we can cultivate a deeper awareness of the interconnectedness of all things, aligning ourselves with the quantum principles that govern the universe and living in a way that reflects the harmony and unity of existence.

Holistic Living: Living the quantum spirituality involves embracing a holistic approach to life, where every aspect of our being—physical, mental, emotional, and spiritual—is aligned with the deeper truths of the quantum field. This means taking care of our bodies through healthy nutrition, exercise, and rest; nurturing our minds through learning, reflection, and creativity; and cultivating our spiritual lives through meditation, prayer, and connection with the divine. By living holistically, we honour the interconnectedness of all aspects of our being, creating a life that is balanced, harmonious, and aligned with the greater rhythms of the universe.

Community and Service: Another key aspect of living the quantum spirituality is the practice of community and service. By engaging with others in meaningful ways and contributing to the well-being of our communities, we reinforce the awareness of our interconnectedness and the importance of collective action. Service can take many forms, from volunteering and activism to simply being present for others in their times of need. By serving others, we align ourselves with the principle of unity and contribute to the creation of a more compassionate and just world.

Continual Growth and Evolution: Finally, living the quantum spirituality involves a commitment to continual growth and evolution. The quantum field is a dynamic, ever-changing reality, and so too must our lives be dynamic and evolving. This means being open to new experiences, learning from our challenges, and constantly seeking to expand our awareness and understanding. By embracing the process of growth and evolution, we align ourselves with the creative forces of the universe, allowing our lives to unfold in ways that reflect our highest potential and purpose.

The Journey of Integration: Embracing Quantum Rituals as a Way of Life

As we conclude this chapter, we are invited to embrace the journey of integration, to incorporate quantum rituals into our daily lives as a way of living the quantum spirituality. This journey is not about abandoning our modern lives or retreating into the past; it is about bringing the wisdom of the ancients into the present, adapting it to the realities of contemporary life, and using it to create a future that honours both science and spirituality.

The journey of integration is a path of continual learning and growth, where we explore the intersections of quantum physics and spirituality, and where we seek to align our lives with the deeper truths of existence. It is a journey that challenges us to live with greater awareness, intention, and creativity, to embrace the quantum rituals that resonate with our soul, and to use them as tools for transformation and alignment.

As we continue our journey into the heart of quantum spirituality, let us carry the wisdom of quantum rituals with us, using them to guide our actions, decisions, and relationships. Let us embrace these sacred practices as a way of living in harmony with the universe and let us use them to create a life that reflects the beauty, balance, and unity of the cosmos.

Quantum rituals offer a powerful way to integrate the principles of quantum physics with spiritual practices, creating a holistic approach to life that honours both the scientific and the sacred. By incorporating these rituals into our daily lives, we can align ourselves with the deeper rhythms of the universe, living in a way that reflects the interconnectedness of all things. As we explore the deeper dimensions of quantum spirituality, we are invited to embrace quantum rituals as a way of living, creating a life that is balanced, harmonious, and aligned with the greater rhythms of existence.

CHAPTER 22: THE QUANTUM MINDFULNESS: MEDITATION AND THE SACRED NOW

In the quiet recesses of the mind, where the boundaries of time dissolve and the past and future fade into the infinite expanse of the present, there exists a profound truth—a truth that has been spoken by sages and mystics throughout the ages. This truth is the power of the sacred now, the realization that the present moment is not just a fleeting point in time, but a gateway to the divine, a portal through which we can connect with the deeper currents of reality. Inspired by Amit Goswami's The Self-Aware Universe, this chapter delves into the practice of quantum mindfulness—a state of being fully present in the sacred now, where meditation and awareness allow us to connect with the quantum field and experience the divine in every moment.

The Sacred Now: The Intersection of Time and Eternity

The present moment, often referred to as the "now," is the only reality we truly experience. The past exists only in memory, and the future is but a projection of the mind. Yet, in the hustle and bustle of modern life, the sacredness of the now is often overlooked, buried beneath the weight of past regrets and future anxieties. Quantum mindfulness invites us to return to the present, to rediscover the divine in the here and now, and to experience the timeless truth that every moment is imbued with sacredness.

Quantum physics offers a fascinating perspective on the nature of time, challenging the linear, deterministic view of the past, present, and future. In the quantum realm, time is not a fixed, unidirectional stream but a fluid, interconnected dimension where all moments are entangled and influence one another. This understanding opens the door to a new way of experiencing time—not as a sequence of events, but as a field of potentiality, where the present moment holds the key to accessing the infinite possibilities of the quantum field.

The sacred now is the point of intersection between time and eternity, the moment where the finite and the infinite meet. It is in this moment that we can connect with the quantum field—the underlying fabric of reality that connects all things. By cultivating quantum mindfulness, we learn to inhabit this moment fully, to open ourselves to the flow of the universe, and to experience the divine presence that permeates every aspect of existence.

Quantum Mindfulness: The Practice of Being Fully Present

Quantum mindfulness is the practice of being fully present in the now, of bringing our awareness to the current moment with intention, clarity, and openness. It is a form of meditation that goes beyond the traditional techniques of concentration and relaxation, inviting us to connect with the deeper dimensions of consciousness and to experience the quantum field in its fullness.

Breath Awareness: One of the simplest and most effective ways to cultivate quantum mindfulness is through breath awareness. The breath is a constant companion, always present, always flowing, and it serves as an anchor that keeps us grounded in the now. By focusing our attention on the breath, we can quiet the mind, calm the nervous system, and bring our awareness to the present moment. Breath awareness helps us to attune to the subtle rhythms of the quantum field, to feel the flow of energy within and around us, and to connect with the divine presence that resides in the heart of the now.

Mindful Observation: Another key practice in quantum mindfulness is mindful observation—the act of observing our thoughts, emotions, and sensations without judgment or attachment. In the quantum realm, the act of observation is not passive; it is an active process that shapes reality. Similarly, in our spiritual lives, the way we observe our inner and outer experiences influences our perception of reality. By practicing mindful observation, we become more aware of the patterns and dynamics that shape our consciousness, allowing us to respond to life with greater clarity, wisdom, and compassion. Mindful observation helps us to see beyond the surface of our experiences, to recognize the deeper truths that lie beneath, and to align ourselves with the flow of the quantum field.

Quantum Meditation: Quantum meditation is a practice that combines traditional meditation techniques with an awareness of the quantum field. In quantum meditation, we enter a state of deep relaxation and openness, where we can connect with the deeper layers of consciousness and experience the interconnectedness of all things. This practice helps us to transcend the limitations of the ego, to dissolve the boundaries between self and other, and to experience the unity of all existence. Quantum meditation allows us to tap into the infinite potentialities of the quantum field, to align ourselves with the divine will, and to create a life that reflects the harmony and balance of the cosmos.

Embodied Presence: Quantum mindfulness is not just a mental or spiritual practice; it is a way of being that involves the whole body. Embodied presence is the practice of bringing our awareness into the body, of feeling the sensations, movements, and energies that flow through us in the present moment. By becoming more attuned to the body, we can experience the sacredness of the now in a more tangible and immediate way. Embodied presence helps us to ground our awareness in the physical world, to feel the connection between the body and the quantum field, and to live with greater vitality, aliveness, and joy.

The Divine Connection: Experiencing the Sacred in Every Moment

The ultimate goal of quantum mindfulness is to experience the divine in every moment, to recognize that the sacred is not something that exists outside of us, but something that is present in the here and now. This experience of the divine is not limited to mystical visions or extraordinary experiences; it is something that can be felt in the simplest of moments, in the breath we take, in the sounds we hear, in the sensations we feel.

Connecting with the Quantum Field: By cultivating quantum mindfulness, we can connect with the quantum field—the underlying reality that connects all things. This connection allows us to experience the unity of all existence, to feel the flow of energy and consciousness that moves through us and the world around us. The quantum field is not something that is separate from us; it is the very fabric of our being, the source of all life and creation. By attuning ourselves to this field, we can experience the divine presence that resides in the heart of the now, and we can align our lives with the deeper rhythms of the universe.

Experiencing the Sacred in the Ordinary: Quantum mindfulness invites us to experience the sacred in the ordinary, to see the divine presence in the everyday moments of life. Whether we are washing the dishes, walking in nature, or sitting in silence, every moment holds the potential for connection with the divine. By bringing our awareness fully into the present moment, we can experience the beauty, mystery, and wonder of life in all its forms. This practice helps us to cultivate a sense of gratitude and reverence for the simple pleasures of life, and to recognize that the sacred is not something that is reserved for special occasions, but something that is present in every moment.

Aligning with the Divine Will: Quantum mindfulness also involves aligning ourselves with the divine will, the higher purpose that guides the flow of the quantum field. This alignment is not about imposing our will on the universe, but about attuning ourselves to the deeper currents of existence and allowing them to guide our actions, decisions, and relationships. By aligning ourselves with the divine will, we can live a life that is in harmony with the universe, creating a reality that reflects the beauty, balance, and unity of the cosmos.

Living in the Sacred Now: The Path of Quantum Mindfulness

Living in the sacred now is the path of quantum mindfulness, a way of life that honours the present moment as the gateway to the divine. This path is not about escaping the realities of the world or withdrawing into a state of detachment; it is about engaging with life fully, with awareness, intention, and presence. It is about recognizing that every moment is an opportunity to connect with the quantum field, to experience the divine, and to create a life that reflects the deeper truths of existence.

Integrating Quantum Mindfulness into Daily Life: The practice of quantum mindfulness is not something that is confined to the meditation cushion or the retreat centre; it is a practice that can be integrated into every aspect of our daily lives. Whether we are at work, at home, or in the community, we can bring the principles of quantum mindfulness into our interactions, decisions, and actions. By doing so, we create a life that is more aligned with the deeper rhythms of the universe, more connected to the quantum field, and more attuned to the sacredness of the now.

Cultivating a Mindful Community: Quantum mindfulness is also a collective practice, one that can be cultivated in community with others. By practicing mindfulness together, we can create a field of awareness that amplifies the energy of the quantum field and deepens our connection to the divine. Whether through group meditation, mindful dialogue, or community service, we can support each other in the practice of living in the sacred now, creating a culture of mindfulness that reflects the unity and harmony of the cosmos.

Embodying the Sacred Now: Finally, the practice of quantum mindfulness invites us to embody the sacred now, to live in a way that reflects the awareness, presence, and connection that we cultivate in our mindfulness practice. This embodiment is not just a mental or spiritual state; it is a way of being that involves the whole body, the whole self, and the whole life. By embodying the sacred now, we become living expressions of the divine, channels through which the quantum field flows into the world, creating a reality that is filled with beauty, love, and grace.

The Journey of Quantum Mindfulness: Embracing the Sacred Now

As we conclude this chapter, we are invited to embrace

the journey of quantum mindfulness, to live in the sacred now, and to experience the divine in every moment. This journey is not about striving for perfection

or attaining some distant goal; it is about returning to the present moment, again and again, with an open heart and an open mind, ready to experience the fullness of life.

The journey of quantum mindfulness is a path of self-discovery, where we explore the depths of our consciousness, connect with the quantum field, and experience the unity of all existence. It is a journey that challenges us to live with greater awareness, intention, and presence, to honour the sacredness of the now, and to align our lives with the deeper rhythms of the universe.

As we continue our journey into the heart of quantum spirituality, let us carry the practice of quantum mindfulness with us, using it to guide our thoughts, actions, and relationships. Let us embrace the sacred now as the gateway to the divine and let us live in a way that reflects the beauty, harmony, and unity of the cosmos.

Quantum mindfulness offers a powerful way to connect with the quantum field and experience the divine in every moment. By practicing mindfulness, meditation, and awareness, we can live in the sacred now, aligning ourselves with the deeper rhythms of the universe and creating a life that reflects the beauty, harmony, and unity of existence. As we explore the deeper dimensions of quantum spirituality, we are invited to embrace quantum mindfulness as a path to experiencing the divine in every moment and living a life that honours the sacredness of the now.

CHAPTER 23: THE SACRED QUANTUM RELATIONSHIPS: LOVE IN THE QUANTUM FIELD

In the intricate dance of the cosmos, where particles intertwine in a delicate and mysterious choreography, there exists a profound truth—a truth that speaks to the deepest aspects of our existence. This truth is the principle of entanglement, a phenomenon where particles, once connected, remain linked across space and time, their destinies intertwined no matter how far they travel. Inspired by Amit Goswami's The Visionary Window, this chapter explores how quantum principles, particularly entanglement, can deepen our relationships and enhance our capacity for love. It invites us to consider how the connections we form with others are not merely physical or emotional, but are also sacred, resonating within the quantum field that underlies all existence.

The Quantum Principle of Entanglement: Interconnection Across Time and Space

Quantum entanglement is one of the most intriguing and enigmatic phenomena in quantum physics. It occurs when two or more particles become linked in such a way that the state of one particle instantaneously influences the state of the other, regardless of the distance separating them. This "spooky action at a distance," as Einstein famously described it, suggests that the universe is far more interconnected than our classical understanding of physics would have us believe.

In the context of relationships, quantum entanglement serves as a powerful metaphor for the deep connections we share with others. Just as entangled particles remain connected across vast distances, so too do the bonds we form with others transcend the limitations of space and time. These connections are not merely the result of shared experiences or mutual affection; they are expressions of a deeper, quantum reality where all beings are interconnected within the fabric of existence.

This understanding challenges us to view our relationships not as isolated interactions, but as part of a larger, interconnected web of life. It invites us to recognize that the love and connection we feel for others are not confined to the physical realm, but resonate within the quantum field, influencing the flow of energy and consciousness in ways that are both profound and mysterious.

Love in the Quantum Field: The Sacred Interconnection of Souls

The concept of love takes on new dimensions when viewed through the lens of quantum entanglement. In this perspective, love is not just an emotion or a feeling; it is a manifestation of the underlying interconnectedness that binds all beings together. Love is the force that draws us into relationship with others, that links our hearts and souls across the distances of space and time, and that allows us to experience the divine presence in the other.

Quantum Love: Quantum love is the recognition that the bonds we share with others are not confined to the material world but extend into the quantum field, where all things are interconnected. This form of love is characterized by a deep sense of unity and oneness, where the boundaries between self and other dissolve, and where the connection we feel is not just emotional or physical, but spiritual and energetic. Quantum love invites us to see our relationships as sacred, as expressions of the divine interconnectedness that permeates all of existence.

Sacred Relationships: In the context of quantum spirituality, relationships are seen as sacred because they reflect the fundamental interconnectedness of all life. When we enter into a relationship with another person, we are not just connecting with their physical or emotional self; we are connecting with their essence, their soul, their quantum being. This understanding invites us to approach our relationships with reverence and respect, recognising that the love we share reflects the divine love that flows through the quantum field.

Sacred relationships honour this interconnectedness, seek to nurture and support the growth of both individuals and recognize the relationship itself as a spiritual journey.

The Resonance of Love: In the quantum field, resonance is a powerful concept that describes how certain frequencies amplify and strengthen each other when they align. In the context of relationships, resonance can be understood as the alignment of energies between two people, where their vibrations harmonize and create a stronger, more coherent bond. Love is the highest form of resonance, where two souls align in such a way that their connection transcends the limitations of the physical world and resonates within the quantum field. This resonance creates a sense of unity and oneness, where the connection between two people becomes a powerful force for healing, growth, and transformation.

Cultivating Quantum Relationships: Practices for Deepening Connections

To cultivate quantum relationships, we must first embrace the understanding that our connections with others are not merely incidental or superficial but are rooted in the deeper reality of the quantum field. This awareness invites us to approach our relationships with a sense of sacredness and intentionality, recognizing that the love we share is a manifestation of the divine interconnectedness that binds all things together.

Mindful Communication: One of the most powerful ways to deepen our relationships is through mindful communication. This practice involves being fully present and attentive when we interact with others, listening not just with our ears, but with our hearts. Mindful communication invites us to go beyond the surface level of conversation and to connect with the deeper essence of the other person. By bringing mindfulness into our interactions, we create a space of openness and receptivity where true connection can flourish. This practice helps us to attune to the energy of the other person, to resonate with their vibration, and to strengthen the quantum bond that links us together.

Intentional Loving-Kindness: Loving-kindness, or metta in the Buddhist tradition, is a practice of cultivating unconditional love and compassion for all beings. When integrated with quantum principles, loving-kindness becomes a powerful tool for deepening our relationships and enhancing our capacity for love. By setting the intention to send loving-kindness to others, we align our consciousness with the quantum field, amplifying the resonance of love and creating a stronger connection with those around us. This practice can be as simple as silently wishing someone well, or as elaborate as a dedicated meditation where we visualize sending love and compassion to all beings. By practicing intentional loving-kindness, we contribute to the creation of a more compassionate and interconnected world.

Shared Meditation and Reflection: Another powerful way to cultivate quantum relationships is through shared meditation and reflection. When two or more people meditate together, they create a shared field of awareness that resonates within the quantum field, amplifying the connection between them. This practice allows us to deepen our bond with others by aligning our energies and intentions, creating a space of unity and oneness. Shared meditation can be followed by a period of reflection, where we discuss our experiences and insights, further strengthening the connection between us. This practice helps us to cultivate a deeper understanding of each other and to create a relationship that is grounded in the sacredness of the quantum field.

Honouring the Sacredness of the Other: In quantum relationships, it is essential to honour the sacredness of the other person, recognizing that they are not just a physical being, but a quantum being, connected to the divine and to the greater whole of existence. This involves treating the other person with respect, compassion, and reverence, recognizing that the love we share reflects the divine love that flows through the quantum field. Honouring the sacredness of the other means seeing them as they truly are—an expression of the divine, a unique and precious being with their own path and purpose. This understanding invites us to support and nurture the growth of the other person, to celebrate their individuality, and to honour the bond we share as a sacred connection within the quantum field.

The Power of Quantum Love: Transforming Relationships and the World

Quantum love is not just a personal experience; it is a transformative force that has the potential to heal and uplift the world. When we cultivate quantum relationships, we contribute to the creation of a more compassionate, interconnected, and spiritually awakened world. The love we share with others ripples out into the quantum field, influencing the collective consciousness and creating a resonance of love that can transform our relationships, our communities, and our planet.

Healing and Transformation: One of the most profound aspects of quantum love is its ability to heal and transform. When we enter into a relationship with another person, we bring our own wounds, fears, and insecurities with us. Quantum love has the power to heal these wounds by creating a space of unconditional acceptance and compassion, where both individuals can be fully seen, heard, and loved. This healing process is not just emotional or psychological; it is also energetic, as the resonance of love within the quantum field has the power to dissolve negative patterns and create new, positive vibrations. By cultivating quantum love, we create relationships that are not only more fulfilling but also more transformative, capable of bringing about profound personal and collective change.

Creating a Resonant Field of Love: Quantum love is not confined to individual relationships; it can also create a resonant field of love that influences the collective consciousness. When we cultivate quantum love, we contribute to the creation of a global field of resonance, where the vibrations of love, compassion, and unity are amplified and strengthened. This resonant field has the power to influence the collective consciousness, creating a ripple effect that can transform the world. By living in alignment with the principles of quantum love, we contribute to the creation of a more loving, compassionate, and interconnected world, where the boundaries between self and other dissolve, and where the unity of all beings is recognized and celebrated.

The Journey of Quantum Relationships: Embracing Love in the Quantum Field

As we conclude this chapter, we are invited to embrace the journey of quantum relationships, to cultivate love in the quantum field, and to deepen our connections with others through the principles of quantum spirituality. This journey is not just about enhancing our personal relationships; it is about contributing to the creation of a more loving, compassionate, and spiritually awakened world.

The journey of quantum relationships is a path of self-discovery, where we explore the depths of our connections with others, recognize the sacredness of our relationships, and experience the transformative power of quantum love. It is a journey that challenges us to live with greater awareness, intention, and compassion, to honour the interconnectedness of all beings, and to align our relationships with the deeper rhythms of the universe.

As we continue our journey into the heart of quantum spirituality, let us carry the principles of quantum relationships with us, using them to guide our interactions, decisions, and connections. Let us embrace quantum love as a path to deeper, more meaningful relationships, and let us contribute to the creation of a world that reflects the beauty, harmony, and unity of the cosmos.

Quantum relationships offer a profound way to deepen our connections with others by recognizing the sacredness of the bonds we share. By cultivating quantum love, we can create relationships that resonate within the quantum field, contributing to the creation of a more compassionate, interconnected, and spiritually awakened world. As we explore the deeper dimensions of quantum spirituality, we are invited to embrace quantum relationships as a path to love, healing, and transformation, both in our personal lives and in the world at large.

CHAPTER 24: THE QUANTUM PATH OF COMPASSION

In the vast, interconnected web of the cosmos, where particles dance in unison and the boundaries between self and other blur into the infinite, there arises a force—gentle yet profound, subtle yet powerful—a force that has the potential to transform not only our relationships with others but also our very understanding of existence. This force is compassion, the deep recognition of our shared humanity and the desire to alleviate the suffering of others. Inspired by The Quantum and the Lotus by Matthieu Ricard and Trinh Xuan Thuan, this chapter explores the role of compassion in the quantum universe. It invites us to consider how the understanding of our interconnectedness through quantum principles can lead us down a path of greater compassion and, ultimately, a more spiritually fulfilling life.

The Interconnectedness of All Things: A Quantum

Understanding

At the heart of quantum physics lies the revelation that everything in the universe is interconnected. The principle of quantum entanglement, which shows that particles once linked remain connected no matter the distance, provides a powerful metaphor for the interconnectedness of all life. In this quantum view, the universe is not a collection of separate, isolated entities but a single, unified field where everything is related, influencing and being influenced by everything else.

This understanding challenges the classical notion of separateness, inviting us to see the world in a new light. If we are all connected, then the boundaries that divide us—our individual identities, our separateness—are illusions, mere constructs of the mind. The suffering of one is, therefore, the suffering of all; the joy of one is the joy of all. This realization is the foundation of compassion, a recognition that the well-being of others is intrinsically linked to our own.

In the quantum universe, compassion is not just a moral imperative or a noble sentiment; it is a natural response to the deep recognition of our interconnectedness. When we understand that we are all part of the same cosmic web, that our actions ripple through the quantum field affecting all beings, we begin to see compassion as an essential quality of an awakened consciousness. It is through compassion that we align ourselves with the deeper rhythms of the universe, fostering harmony, balance, and peace within the quantum field.

The Nature of Quantum Compassion: A Path to Spiritual Fulfilment

Quantum compassion is more than just empathy or kindness; it is a profound understanding that arises from the recognition of our shared existence within the quantum field. This type of compassion is rooted in the awareness that we are not separate from others, that the boundaries between "self" and "other" are fluid and permeable, shaped by the same fundamental forces that govern the universe.

The Flow of Compassion in the Quantum Field: In the quantum universe, compassion can be seen as a flow of energy, a vibration that resonates within the quantum field and influences the interconnected web of life. When we act with compassion, we align ourselves with this flow, contributing to the creation of positive energy that ripples outward, affecting others in ways that we may not immediately see or understand. This flow of compassion is not limited by space or time; it transcends the physical world, resonating within the quantum field and influencing the collective consciousness.

Compassion as a Bridge to the Divine: In many spiritual traditions, compassion is seen as a bridge to the divine, a way of connecting with the sacred essence of life. In the context of quantum spirituality, compassion takes on an even deeper significance, as it reflects the fundamental interconnectedness of all things. By practicing compassion, we tap into the divine flow of the universe, aligning ourselves with the higher frequencies of love, unity, and harmony. This alignment brings us closer to the divine, allowing us to experience the presence of the sacred in our daily lives and to live in a way that reflects the beauty and unity of the cosmos.

The Role of Compassion in Spiritual Fulfilment: Spiritual fulfilment is often described as a state of inner peace, contentment, and connection with the divine. Compassion plays a central role in achieving this fulfilment, as it helps us to transcend the ego-driven desires and fears that often dominate our lives. By cultivating compassion, we open our hearts to others, breaking down the barriers that separate us and allowing us to experience the deep interconnectedness of all life. This experience of interconnectedness is the essence of spiritual fulfilment, as it allows us to live in harmony with the universe and to contribute to the well-being of all beings.

Cultivating Quantum Compassion: Practices for a Compassionate Life

To walk the quantum path of compassion, we must first cultivate the awareness of our interconnectedness and develop practices that help us to embody compassion in our daily lives. These practices are not just about feeling compassion but about living it, about making compassion a central part of our way of being in the world.

Mindful Awareness of Interconnectedness: The first step in cultivating quantum compassion is to develop a mindful awareness of our interconnectedness with all beings. This awareness can be cultivated through meditation, reflection, and contemplation on the nature of the quantum field and our place within it. By regularly reminding ourselves that we are all connected, that our actions have an impact on others, we can deepen our sense of responsibility and care for the well-being of all beings. This practice helps us to see beyond the illusion of separateness and to recognize the shared humanity that unites us all.

Loving-Kindness Meditation: Loving-kindness meditation, or metta meditation, is a powerful practice for cultivating compassion. In this practice, we silently repeat phrases of loving-kindness, first for ourselves, then for others, and finally for all beings. By sending out vibrations of love and compassion into the quantum field, we contribute to the creation of a more compassionate and harmonious world. This practice not only benefits others but also helps to soften our hearts, dissolving the barriers that separate us from others and deepening our capacity for empathy and compassion.

Compassionate Action: Compassion is not just a feeling; it is a way of living that manifests in our actions. To cultivate quantum compassion, we must make a conscious effort to act with kindness, empathy, and care in our daily lives. This might involve helping someone in need, listening deeply to a friend, or standing up for justice and fairness. By acting with compassion, we align ourselves with the flow of the quantum field, contributing to the creation of positive energy that resonates within the interconnected web of life. Compassionate action is not just about doing good deeds; it is about living in a way that reflects our awareness of interconnectedness and our commitment to the well-being of all beings.

Gratitude as a Path to Compassion: Gratitude is closely linked to compassion, as it helps us to recognize the blessings we receive from others and the interconnectedness that supports our lives. By cultivating a sense of gratitude, we open our hearts to others, deepening our capacity for compassion and kindness. Gratitude helps us to see the world through the lens of abundance rather than scarcity, recognizing the many ways in which we are supported by the universe and by the people in our lives. This recognition fosters a sense of humility and a desire to give back, to contribute to the well-being of others as an expression of our gratitude.

The Transformative Power of Compassion: Creating a Compassionate World

Compassion is not just a personal virtue; it is a transformative force that has the power to change the world. When we cultivate quantum compassion, we contribute to the creation of a more compassionate and just society, where the well-being of all beings is recognized and honoured.

Healing the Collective Consciousness: One of the most profound effects of compassion is its ability to heal the collective consciousness. In a world that is often characterized by division, conflict, and suffering, compassion acts as a healing balm, soothing the wounds of the past and creating a foundation for a more peaceful and harmonious future. By practicing compassion, we contribute to the creation of a collective consciousness that is rooted in love, unity, and interconnectedness. This healing process is not just emotional or psychological; it is also energetic, as the resonance of compassion within the quantum field has the power to transform negative patterns and create new, positive vibrations.

Building Compassionate Communities: Compassion

is also essential for building strong, supportive communities. When we practice compassion in our relationships with others, we create a culture of care and respect, where the well-being of all members is prioritized. Compassionate communities are those that recognize the interconnectedness of all beings and work together to create a world that reflects this awareness. By fostering a sense of belonging and connection, compassionate communities contribute to the creation of a more just and equitable society, where everyone has the opportunity to thrive.

Inspiring Global Compassion: Finally, quantum compassion has the potential to inspire a global movement towards greater compassion and understanding. In a world that is increasingly interconnected, both physically and energetically, the need for compassion has never been greater. By living the quantum path of compassion, we inspire others to do the same, creating a ripple effect that can spread across the globe. This global movement towards compassion has the power to transform our world, creating a future where the well-being of all beings is recognized and honoured, and where the unity of all life is celebrated.

Walking the Quantum Path of Compassion: A Journey of Transformation

As we conclude this chapter, we are invited to walk the quantum path of compassion, to cultivate a deep awareness of our interconnectedness, and to live in a way that reflects this understanding. This journey is not just about feeling compassion; it is about embodying compassion in our thoughts, actions, and relationships, and about contributing to the creation of a more compassionate and just world.

The quantum path of compassion is a journey of self-discovery, where we explore the depths of our capacity for love and care, and where we recognize the sacredness of all beings. It is a journey that challenges us to live with greater awareness, intention, and kindness, to honour the interconnectedness of all life, and to align ourselves with the deeper rhythms of the universe.

As we continue our journey into the heart of quantum spirituality, let us carry the principles of quantum compassion with us, using them to guide our actions, decisions, and relationships. Let us embrace compassion as a path to deeper spiritual fulfilment and as a way of contributing to the creation of a world that reflects the beauty, harmony, and unity of the cosmos.

Quantum compassion offers a powerful way to live in alignment with the interconnectedness of the quantum universe. By cultivating compassion in our daily lives, we can create a more compassionate and spiritually fulfilling world, where the well-being of all beings is recognized and honoured. As we explore the deeper dimensions of quantum spirituality, we are invited to embrace compassion as a path to spiritual fulfilment and as a way of contributing to the creation of a more just and compassionate world.

CHAPTER 25: THE SACRED ART OF QUANTUM CREATION

In the boundless expanse of the universe, where the unseen forces of energy and consciousness weave the intricate patterns of reality, there exists a profound power—a power that lies within each of us, waiting to be awakened. This power is the art of quantum creation, the ability to manifest reality through the alignment of intention and spiritual awareness with the quantum field. Inspired by Lynne McTaggart's The Field, this chapter explores the sacred process of quantum creation, offering practical guidance on how to harness this power to create a life that reflects the divine. It invites us to step into our role as co-creators with the universe, using the principles of quantum physics and spirituality to shape our reality in harmony with the greater cosmic order.

The Quantum Field: The Source of Infinite Possibility

At the heart of quantum physics lies the concept of the quantum field—a vast, invisible matrix that underlies all of existence, connecting every particle, every atom, every being in a web of energy and information. The quantum field is not just a passive backdrop to the material world; it is the source of all potential, the realm where possibilities are born and where reality takes shape.

In this field, everything that exists is interconnected, and the boundaries between the observer and the observed, between mind and matter, begin to dissolve. This understanding challenges the classical view of a fixed, deterministic universe, revealing instead a reality that is fluid, dynamic, and responsive to consciousness. The quantum field is a realm of infinite possibility, where every thought, every intention, every action has the power to influence the unfolding of reality.

Quantum creation is the process of consciously engaging with the quantum field, using the power of intention and spiritual alignment to manifest the reality we desire. It is the recognition that we are not merely passive observers of the universe, but active participants in the creation of our lives. By aligning our thoughts, emotions, and actions with the deeper rhythms of the quantum field, we can create a life that reflects the divine, a life that is in harmony with the greater cosmic order.

The Process of Quantum Creation: Aligning with the Divine

The process of quantum creation begins with the recognition of our inherent connection to the quantum field and our role as co-creators with the universe. This process involves several key steps, each of which is essential for manifesting reality in alignment with the divine.

Setting Clear Intentions: The first step in quantum creation is setting clear, focused intentions. In the quantum field, intentions act as a powerful force, directing the flow of energy and shaping the potentialities that exist within the field. By setting a clear intention, we send a signal into the quantum field, aligning ourselves with the outcomes we wish to manifest. This intention must be specific, positive, and aligned with our highest values and spiritual aspirations. It is important to approach this step with clarity and purpose, recognizing that our intentions have the power to influence the reality we experience.

Cultivating Spiritual Alignment: The next step in the process of quantum creation is cultivating spiritual alignment. This involves aligning our thoughts, emotions, and actions with the higher frequencies of love, compassion, and unity that resonate within the quantum field. Spiritual alignment is about tuning into the deeper rhythms of the universe, allowing our intentions to be guided by the divine will rather than by ego-driven desires. This step requires us to cultivate a state of openness, receptivity, and trust, recognizing that the universe is always moving in the direction of growth, evolution, and harmony. By aligning ourselves with these higher frequencies, we create a resonance with the quantum field that amplifies the power of our intentions and supports the manifestation of our desired reality.

Visualization and Imagination: Visualization is a

powerful tool for quantum creation, as it allows us to connect with the quantum field and bring our intentions into focus. By visualizing our desired outcomes with clarity and detail, we create a mental image that acts as a blueprint for the reality we wish to manifest. This visualization should be vivid and emotionally charged, as the energy of our emotions amplifies the signal we send into the quantum field. Imagination plays a crucial role in this process, as it allows us to explore the infinite possibilities that exist within the quantum field and to create a vision that is aligned with our highest potential.

Embodying the Desired Reality: Another key aspect of quantum creation is the practice of embodying the desired reality. This involves acting as if our desired outcomes have already been realized, aligning our thoughts, emotions, and behaviours with the reality we wish to create. By embodying the desired reality, we create a resonance with the quantum field that attracts the circumstances, opportunities, and resources needed to bring our vision into manifestation. This step requires us to let go of doubt and fear and to fully commit to the reality we wish to create, trusting that the universe will support us in the fulfilment of our intentions.

Practicing Gratitude and Detachment: Gratitude is a powerful force in the process of quantum creation, as it aligns us with the frequency of abundance and amplifies the energy of our intentions. By cultivating a sense of gratitude for the blessings we have received and for the reality we are in the process of manifesting, we create a positive feedback loop that reinforces our connection to the quantum field. At the same time, it is important to practice detachment, releasing our attachment to specific outcomes and trusting that the universe will manifest our desires in the way that is most aligned with our highest good. Detachment does not mean giving up on our intentions; it means surrendering to the flow of the universe and allowing the quantum field to bring forth the best possible outcome.

The Power of Quantum Creation: Manifesting a Divine Life

The art of quantum creation is a powerful tool for manifesting a life that reflects the divine. By consciously engaging with the quantum field and aligning our intentions with the higher frequencies of the universe, we can create a reality that is in harmony with the greater cosmic order. This process is not about forcing our will upon the universe; it is about co-creating with the divine, allowing our intentions to be guided by the deeper wisdom of the quantum field.

Manifesting Abundance: One of the most common desires in the process of quantum creation is the manifestation of abundance—whether in the form of financial prosperity, health, relationships, or personal fulfilment. Abundance is a natural state of the universe, and by aligning ourselves with the frequency of abundance, we can attract the resources, opportunities, and experiences that support our highest good. This requires us to cultivate a mindset of abundance, recognizing that the universe is infinitely generous and that we are deserving of the blessings we seek. By focusing on what we desire rather than on what we lack, we create a resonance with the quantum field that attracts abundance into our lives.

Creating Harmonious Relationships: Quantum creation can also be used to manifest harmonious and fulfilling relationships. By setting clear intentions for the types of relationships we wish to experience and aligning ourselves with the frequency of love and compassion, we can attract people into our lives who resonate with our values and aspirations. This process involves being mindful of the energy we bring into our relationships, practicing kindness, empathy, and respect, and embodying the qualities we wish to see in others. By creating a positive resonance with the quantum field, we can cultivate relationships that are supportive, loving, and aligned with our spiritual path.

Fulfilling Life Purpose: Another powerful application of quantum creation is the manifestation of our life purpose. By setting clear intentions for our spiritual and personal growth, and by aligning ourselves with the divine will, we can attract the opportunities and resources needed to fulfil our highest potential. This process involves connecting with our inner guidance, listening to the whispers of the soul, and taking inspired action towards our goals. By trusting in the flow of the universe and remaining open to the possibilities that arise, we can manifest a life that is deeply fulfilling and aligned with our true purpose.

The Journey of Quantum Creation: Living as Co-Creators with the Universe

As we conclude this chapter, we are invited to embrace the journey of quantum creation, to step into our role as co-creators with the universe, and to manifest a life that reflects the divine. This journey is not just about achieving external success or material wealth; it is about aligning ourselves with the deeper rhythms of the quantum field and creating a reality that is in harmony with the greater cosmic order.

The journey of quantum creation is a path of self-discovery, where we explore the power of our intentions, the wisdom of the quantum field, and the sacred process of manifesting reality. It is a journey that challenges us to live with greater awareness, intention, and alignment, to honour the interconnectedness of all things, and to create a life that reflects the beauty, harmony, and unity of the cosmos.

As we continue our journey into the heart of quantum spirituality, let us carry the principles of quantum creation with us, using them to guide our thoughts, actions, and decisions. Let us embrace the sacred art of quantum creation as a way of manifesting a life that reflects the divine and let us live in a way that honours our role as co-creators with the universe.

Quantum creation offers a powerful way to manifest reality through intention and spiritual alignment with the quantum field. By consciously engaging with the quantum field and aligning our intentions with the divine will, we can create a life that reflects the beauty, harmony, and unity of the cosmos. As we explore the deeper dimensions of quantum spirituality, we are invited to embrace the sacred art of quantum creation as a path to living in harmony with the universe and manifesting a reality that reflects our highest potential and spiritual aspirations.

CHAPTER 26: THE QUANTUM EVOLUTION: A NEW VISION FOR HUMANITY

In the stillness of the cosmos, where the whispers of ancient wisdom meet the cutting-edge revelations of modern science, there lies a potential so vast, so transformative, that it has the power to reshape the very fabric of our existence. This potential is the quantum evolution of humanity—a process through which the integration of quantum science and spirituality could lead us to a new era of enlightenment and harmony. Inspired by Ervin Laszlo's Science and the Akashic Field, this chapter explores the possibility of a future where humanity evolves beyond its current limitations, embracing a new vision of existence that honours both the material and the mystical, the scientific and the sacred.

The Akashic Field: The Blueprint of Evolution

At the core of Ervin Laszlo's work is the concept of the Akashic Field—a universal field of information that underlies and connects all things. This field, often described as the "cosmic memory" or the "field of all possibilities," is believed to store the knowledge of the past, present, and future, acting as a blueprint for the evolution of the universe and all beings within it. In this view, the Akashic Field is not just a repository of information, but a dynamic, living field that guides the unfolding of reality and the evolution of consciousness.

In the context of quantum evolution, the Akashic Field represents the potential for humanity to access higher levels of knowledge and awareness, to tap into the deeper truths of existence, and to align our collective evolution with the greater cosmic order. This field is a bridge between science and spirituality, offering a framework through which we can understand the interconnectedness of all things and the role of consciousness in shaping reality.

The Akashic Field suggests that evolution is not a random, chaotic process, but a purposeful, intelligent unfolding guided by the deeper rhythms of the universe. It invites us to consider the possibility that humanity is on the brink of a quantum leap in evolution—a shift from a purely materialistic worldview to one that embraces the spiritual dimensions of existence, leading to a more enlightened and harmonious future.

The Quantum Leap: Humanity's Evolutionary Potential

The concept of a quantum leap—a sudden, dramatic shift in state—is a powerful metaphor for the potential evolution of humanity. Just as particles in the quantum realm can leap from one state to another without passing through intermediate states, so too could humanity undergo a rapid and profound transformation, shifting from a state of fragmentation and conflict to one of unity and harmony.

Integration of Science and Spirituality: The integration of quantum science and spirituality is key to this evolutionary leap. Quantum science, with its revelations of interconnectedness, non-locality, and the role of consciousness in shaping reality, offers a new understanding of the universe that aligns closely with ancient spiritual teachings. By integrating these two domains, humanity can move beyond the dualistic thinking that has dominated much of our history—thinking that separates mind from matter, science from spirituality, and self from other. This integration opens the door to a more holistic, unified vision of existence, where the material and the mystical are seen as complementary aspects of the same underlying reality.

Expansion of Consciousness: Quantum evolution also involves the expansion of consciousness, both individually and collectively. As we become more aware of the deeper dimensions of reality, we begin to transcend the ego-driven, materialistic mindset that has often led to conflict, exploitation, and environmental degradation. This expanded consciousness allows us to see beyond our individual concerns, recognizing our interconnectedness with all life and our responsibility to care for the planet and each other. The expansion of consciousness is not just about acquiring new knowledge; it is about developing new ways of being—ways that are aligned with the principles of love, compassion, and unity.

The Emergence of a Global Consciousness: One of the most profound aspects of quantum evolution is the emergence of a global consciousness—a collective awareness that transcends national, cultural, and religious boundaries. This global consciousness is rooted in the recognition of our shared humanity and our interconnectedness with the Earth and the cosmos. It is a consciousness that seeks to create a world that reflects the principles of justice, peace, and sustainability, where the well-being of all beings is prioritized. The emergence of a global consciousness represents a quantum leap in humanity's evolution, as it involves a fundamental shift in how we see ourselves and our place in the world.

A New Vision for Humanity: The Quantum Future

The potential for quantum evolution offers a new vision for humanity—a vision of a future where the integration of quantum science and spirituality leads to a more enlightened and harmonious world. This vision is not a utopian fantasy, but a realistic possibility that is already beginning to unfold as more people awaken to the deeper truths of existence and embrace the principles of quantum spirituality.

A World of Interconnectedness and Unity: In the quantum future, the recognition of our interconnectedness will lead to a world where unity and cooperation are valued over division and competition.

This shift in consciousness will transform our social, political, and economic systems, creating structures that are more inclusive, equitable, and sustainable. In this future, the well-being of all beings will be seen as interconnected, and policies and practices will be guided by the principles of compassion, justice, and stewardship of the Earth. This vision of interconnectedness and unity is not just an abstract ideal; it is a practical guide for creating a world that reflects the deeper rhythms of the universe.

A Culture of Consciousness and Creativity: The quantum future also envisions a culture that values consciousness and creativity as central aspects of human life. In this future, education, art, and science will be integrated in ways that foster the development of the whole person —mind, body, and spirit. Creativity will be seen as a form of co-creation with the universe, a way of bringing the infinite possibilities of the quantum field into manifestation. This culture of consciousness and creativity will encourage individuals to explore their inner worlds, to develop their unique gifts and talents, and to contribute to the collective evolution of humanity.

A Relationship with the Earth and the Cosmos: In the quantum future, humanity's relationship with the Earth and the cosmos will be transformed. The recognition of our interconnectedness with all life will lead to a renewed sense of stewardship for the planet, where the health and well-being of the Earth are prioritized. This shift in consciousness will lead to the development of sustainable technologies and practices that support the regeneration of the planet's ecosystems. Additionally, humanity will begin to explore its relationship with the cosmos, not just as a physical space to be explored, but as a living, conscious reality with which we are deeply connected. This cosmic relationship will inspire new forms of spirituality, art, and science, as we seek to understand our place in the greater universe.

The Path to Quantum Evolution: Practical Steps for the Future

The realization of this quantum future requires more than just vision; it requires action. The path to quantum evolution involves practical steps that individuals, communities, and societies can take to align themselves with the principles of quantum spirituality and to contribute to the collective evolution of humanity.

Cultivating Personal and Collective Awareness: The first step on the path to quantum evolution is the cultivation of personal and collective awareness. This involves developing a deeper understanding of the principles of quantum science and spirituality and applying these principles in our daily lives. It also involves creating spaces for collective reflection, dialogue, and action, where individuals can come together to explore the implications of quantum spirituality and to develop strategies for creating a more enlightened and harmonious world.

Promoting Education and Integration: Education is key to the realization of the quantum future. This involves not only teaching the principles of quantum science and spirituality but also integrating these principles into all aspects of education—from early childhood through to higher education. By promoting education that fosters critical thinking, creativity, and spiritual awareness, we can prepare future generations to take on the challenges of the quantum future and to contribute to the collective evolution of humanity.

Building Communities of Practice: The path to quantum evolution also involves the creation of communities of practice—groups of individuals who are committed to living the principles of quantum spirituality in their daily lives. These communities can serve as models of what is possible when people come together with a shared vision of a more enlightened and harmonious world. They can also serve as centres of innovation and experimentation, where new ideas and practices are developed and tested. By building communities of practice, we can create networks of support and collaboration that will be essential for the realization of the quantum future.

Engaging in Global Transformation: Finally, the path to quantum evolution requires us to engage in global transformation—to work towards the creation of a world that reflects the principles of quantum spirituality. This involves not only addressing the pressing social, economic, and environmental challenges of our time but also creating new systems and structures that support the emergence of a more enlightened and harmonious world. Global transformation requires a collective effort, where individuals, communities, and societies come together to co-create the quantum future.

The Journey of Quantum Evolution: Embracing the Future

As we conclude this chapter, we are invited to embrace the journey of quantum evolution, to envision a future where the integration of quantum science and spirituality leads to a more enlightened and harmonious world. This journey is not just about envisioning the future; it is about taking practical steps to bring this vision into reality.

The journey of quantum evolution is a path of collective awakening, where humanity recognizes its interconnectedness with all life and begins to live in alignment with the deeper rhythms of the universe. It is a journey that challenges us to expand our consciousness, to integrate science and spirituality, and to co-create a future that reflects the beauty, harmony, and unity of the cosmos.

As we continue our journey into the heart of quantum spirituality, let us carry the vision of quantum evolution with us, using it to guide our actions, decisions, and relationships. Let us embrace the sacred future as a path to collective enlightenment and let us work together to create a world that reflects the divine order of the universe.

Quantum evolution offers a new vision for humanity, where the integration of quantum science and spirituality leads to a more enlightened and harmonious world. By embracing the principles of quantum spirituality and taking practical steps to bring this vision into reality, we can contribute to the collective evolution of humanity and create a future that reflects the beauty, harmony, and unity of the cosmos. As we explore the deeper dimensions of quantum spirituality, we are invited to embrace quantum evolution as a path to collective awakening and to work together to create the sacred future.

CHAPTER 27: THE QUANTUM LEGACY: PASSING THE TORCH TO FUTURE GENERATIONS

In the quiet moments between the past and the future, where the wisdom of the ages meets the infinite potential of what is yet to come, there lies a profound responsibility—a responsibility to ensure that the knowledge and insights we have gained are not lost, but carried forward, illuminating the path for those who will follow. This responsibility is the essence of the quantum legacy—the torch that we pass to future generations, a legacy that honours both scientific and spiritual truths, and guides humanity toward a more enlightened and harmonious future. Inspired by Gregg Braden's The Divine Matrix, this chapter explores how we can cultivate and transmit this quantum legacy, ensuring that the integration of quantum science and spirituality continues to inspire, guide, and uplift those who come after us.

The Power of Legacy: Shaping the Future Through the Present

Legacy is often thought of as something material—wealth, property, or status passed down from one generation to the next. But the quantum legacy is something far more profound; it is the transmission of knowledge, wisdom, and values that shape the consciousness of future generations. In the context of quantum spirituality, this legacy is rooted in the understanding of our interconnectedness with all life, our role as co-creators with the universe, and our commitment to living in alignment with the deeper rhythms of existence.

The quantum legacy is not just about preserving knowledge; it is about cultivating a living tradition that evolves and adapts over time. It is about fostering a sense of continuity and connection, where each generation builds upon the insights and achievements of the previous ones, contributing to the collective evolution of humanity. This legacy is not static or fixed; it is dynamic, growing and expanding as we deepen our understanding of the quantum field and our place within it.

The Role of the Divine Matrix: At the heart of this legacy is the concept of the Divine Matrix, a field of energy and information that connects all things. The Divine Matrix is not just a backdrop to reality; it is the medium through which our thoughts, intentions, and actions influence the world around us. By understanding and working with the Divine Matrix, we can consciously shape the future, creating a legacy that reflects the highest aspirations of humanity. This requires us to be mindful of the energy we contribute to the Matrix, recognizing that our every thought, word, and deed resonates within this field, influencing the unfolding of reality.

The Intergenerational Transmission of Wisdom: The quantum legacy is also about the intergenerational transmission of wisdom. This involves not only passing down knowledge and insights but also fostering the values and practices that will enable future generations to thrive. It requires us to be intentional in how we educate and inspire those who come after us, ensuring that they are equipped with the tools and understanding needed to navigate the complexities of the quantum world. This transmission is not limited to formal education; it occurs in the stories we tell, the traditions we uphold, and the example we set in our daily lives.

Cultivating the Quantum Legacy: Practical Steps for Future Generations

To cultivate a quantum legacy that honours both scientific and spiritual truths, we must take deliberate and thoughtful steps to ensure that this knowledge is preserved, expanded, and transmitted to future generations. This involves a combination of education, practice, and community building, all aimed at fostering a deep and enduring connection to the principles of quantum spirituality.

Integrating Quantum Spirituality into Education: One of the most important steps in cultivating the quantum legacy is integrating quantum spirituality into education. This means going beyond traditional curricula to include teachings that explore the interconnectedness of all life, the role of consciousness in shaping reality, and the integration of science and spirituality. Education should be holistic, addressing the intellectual, emotional, and spiritual development of students. By introducing these concepts at an early age, we can help future generations develop a deeper understanding of the quantum field and their role as co-creators with the universe.

Mentorship and Guidance: Mentorship plays a crucial role in the transmission of the quantum legacy. Those who have gained insight into quantum spirituality have a responsibility to guide and mentor the younger generation, helping them to navigate the challenges and opportunities of the quantum world. This mentorship involves not only sharing knowledge but also modelling the values and practices that embody quantum spirituality. By fostering relationships based on mutual respect, curiosity, and a shared commitment to growth, mentors can help cultivate a new generation of quantum thinkers who are equipped to carry the torch forward.

Creating Communities of Practice: Another key aspect of cultivating the quantum legacy is the creation of communities of practice. These are groups of individuals who come together to explore, practice, and live the principles of quantum spirituality. Communities of practice provide a supportive environment where individuals can learn from one another, share insights, and collaborate on projects that embody the values of quantum spirituality. By fostering a sense of belonging and connection, these communities help to ensure that the quantum legacy is not only preserved but also evolves and adapts over time.

Encouraging Creative Expression: Creative expression is a powerful tool for transmitting the quantum legacy. Whether through art, music, writing, or other forms of creative expression, individuals can explore and communicate the principles of quantum spirituality in ways that resonate deeply with others. Encouraging creative expression allows future generations to engage with these concepts in a personal and meaningful way, fostering a deeper connection to the quantum field and their role within it. By celebrating and supporting creativity, we help to ensure that the quantum legacy remains vibrant and alive.

Preserving and Sharing Knowledge: Finally, it is essential to preserve and share the knowledge of quantum spirituality in ways that are accessible to future generations. This involves documenting insights, experiences, and practices, and making them available through various mediums—books, digital platforms, workshops, and more. It also involves creating spaces where knowledge can be shared and discussed, fostering an ongoing dialogue that keeps the legacy of quantum spirituality dynamic and relevant. By ensuring that this knowledge is preserved and shared, we help to create a foundation upon which future generations can build.

The Future of the Quantum Legacy: A Vision of Hope and Possibility

The quantum legacy we cultivate today will shape the world of tomorrow. By integrating quantum science and spirituality, we can create a future that is more enlightened, compassionate, and harmonious. This future is one where the principles of interconnectedness, unity, and love guide our actions and decisions, leading to a world that reflects the beauty and order of the cosmos.

A World Guided by Wisdom and Compassion: In the future envisioned by the quantum legacy, wisdom and compassion will be the guiding principles of human society. The understanding of our interconnectedness will lead to policies and practices that prioritize the well-being of all beings, fostering a culture of care and respect. This will be a world where differences are celebrated, where diversity is seen as a strength, and where collaboration and cooperation are the norm. By embracing wisdom and compassion, future generations will create a society that is just, equitable, and sustainable.

The Evolution of Consciousness: The quantum legacy also envisions the continued evolution of human consciousness. As more people awaken to the deeper truths of quantum spirituality, there will be a collective shift towards higher states of awareness and understanding. This evolution of consciousness will lead to new ways of thinking, being, and relating, transforming not only individual lives but also the structures and systems that govern society. The continued evolution of consciousness will be a key driver of the quantum legacy, ensuring that future generations are equipped to navigate the complexities of the quantum world.

A Legacy of Hope and Possibility: Ultimately, the quantum legacy is a legacy of hope and possibility. It is a reminder that we are not bound by the limitations of the past but are free to create a future that reflects our highest aspirations. By embracing the principles of quantum spirituality, we can create a world that is filled with beauty, harmony, and unity—a world that reflects the divine order of the universe. This legacy is not just a gift to future generations; it is a responsibility we all share, a responsibility to ensure that the light of quantum spirituality continues to shine, guiding humanity towards a future of hope and possibility.

Embracing the Quantum Legacy: A Call to Action

As we conclude this final chapter, we are called to embrace the quantum legacy, to take up the torch and carry it forward for the sake of future generations. This is not a passive inheritance; it is an active, living tradition that requires our commitment, our creativity, and our courage. By embracing the quantum legacy, we commit ourselves to living the principles of quantum spirituality, to sharing this knowledge with others, and to contributing to the collective evolution of humanity.

The journey of quantum spirituality is a journey of discovery, of awakening, and of transformation. It is a journey that challenges us to live with greater awareness, intention, and alignment with the deeper rhythms of the universe. As we continue this journey, let us remember that we are not alone; we are part of a vast, interconnected web of life, a cosmic dance that has been unfolding for eons and will continue to unfold long after we are gone.

Let us embrace the quantum legacy with joy and gratitude, knowing that by doing so, we are contributing to a future that is filled with hope, possibility, and light.

And let us pass this torch to future generations, ensuring that the wisdom of quantum spirituality continues to inspire, guide, and uplift all who come after us.

The quantum legacy is a profound responsibility and a gift, one that we are called to cultivate, preserve, and pass on to future generations. By integrating quantum science and spirituality, we can create a legacy that reflects the beauty, harmony, and unity of the cosmos, guiding humanity towards a more enlightened and harmonious future. As we explore the deeper dimensions of quantum spirituality, we are invited to embrace the quantum legacy as a call to action, a call to contribute to the collective evolution of humanity and to create a world that reflects the divine order of the universe.

CHAPTER 28: THE SACRED SYMPHONY: HARMONIZING SCIENCE AND SPIRIT IN THE WORLD

In the vast, resonant spaces of the cosmos, where the laws of physics and the mysteries of spirit intertwine in a dance of creation, there echoes a symphony—a sacred symphony that encompasses all of existence. This symphony is not composed of notes and rhythms, but of the fundamental principles that govern the universe, the deep patterns that underlie both the material and the mystical. Inspired by David Bohm's Wholeness and the

Implicate Order, this chapter explores the idea of a sacred symphony—a harmonious integration of science and spirit in the world. It invites us to consider how we can contribute to this symphony by living in alignment with quantum principles and spiritual values, creating a life that reflects the unity, beauty, and order of the cosmos.

The Implicate Order: The Hidden Harmony of the Universe

David Bohm's concept of the Implicate Order offers a profound insight into the nature of reality. According to Bohm, the universe is not a collection of separate, independent parts, but a unified whole where everything is interconnected and enfolded within a deeper, underlying order. This Implicate Order is the source from which all forms and phenomena emerge, an invisible matrix that gives rise to the explicit, manifest world we experience.

In this view, reality is like a symphony, where each note and phrase is part of a greater, harmonious whole. The Implicate Order is the score, the underlying structure that guides the unfolding of the universe, while the explicit order—the world of matter and energy—is the music that we perceive. This metaphor invites us to see the universe not as a chaotic, random system, but as a sacred symphony, where science and spirit are not separate domains but are intimately connected aspects of the same reality.

The idea of the Implicate Order challenges us to rethink our understanding of science and spirituality. It suggests that the material world is not isolated from the spiritual, but is an expression of the deeper, hidden order that permeates all of existence. This understanding opens the door to a new way of living, where we align ourselves with the harmony of the universe and contribute to the sacred symphony that unfolds in every moment.

Harmonizing Science and Spirit: The Sacred Integration

The integration of science and spirituality is at the heart of the sacred symphony. This integration is not about merging two separate disciplines, but about recognizing that they are different expressions of the same underlying reality. Science seeks to understand the laws and patterns that govern the material world, while spirituality seeks to connect with the deeper truths and meanings that give life its sacredness. When these two perspectives are brought together, they create a harmonious, holistic understanding of the universe, where the material and the mystical are seen as complementary aspects of the same cosmic dance.

Living in Alignment with Quantum Principles: One of the ways we can contribute to the sacred symphony is by living in alignment with quantum principles. Quantum physics reveals a universe that is interconnected, dynamic, and responsive to consciousness. By embracing these principles in our daily lives, we can cultivate a deeper awareness of the interconnectedness of all things and make choices that reflect this understanding. This involves being mindful of the impact of our thoughts, actions, and intentions, recognizing that they resonate within the quantum field and influence the unfolding of reality. Living in alignment with quantum principles means embracing the fluidity and potentiality of life, being open to change and transformation, and trusting in the deeper order that guides the universe.

Embodying Spiritual Values: Alongside the quantum principles, spiritual values such as love, compassion, and unity are essential components of the sacred symphony. These values are not just abstract ideals; they are the qualities that resonate most deeply with the harmony of the universe. By embodying these values in our relationships, work, and communities, we contribute to the creation of a more harmonious and compassionate world. This involves cultivating a sense of reverence for life, seeing the sacred in all beings, and acting with kindness and empathy. Spiritual values are the heart of the sacred symphony, guiding us to live in a way that honours the interconnectedness of all existence.

The Dance of Science and Spirit: The sacred symphony is not static; it is a dynamic, evolving dance where science and spirit continually interact and inform each other. This dance invites us to explore the mysteries of the universe with both the rigor of scientific inquiry and the openness of spiritual contemplation. It challenges us to expand our understanding of reality, to seek knowledge not just with our minds but with our hearts, and to integrate the insights of science with the wisdom of spiritual traditions. By participating in this dance, we contribute to the unfolding of the sacred symphony, adding our unique voice to the chorus of creation.

Contributing to the Sacred Symphony: Practical Steps for Harmonious Living

Contributing to the sacred symphony requires more than just understanding; it requires action. This action is not about grand gestures or dramatic changes; it is about the small, everyday choices we make that align us with the harmony of the universe. Here are some practical steps we can take to contribute to the sacred symphony:

Cultivating Awareness and Presence: The first step in contributing to the sacred symphony is cultivating awareness and presence. This involves being fully present in each moment, aware of our thoughts, emotions, and surroundings. By cultivating mindfulness, we can tune into the deeper rhythms of life and make choices that are aligned with the harmony of the universe. This practice helps us to become more attuned to the interconnectedness of all things and to respond to life's challenges with wisdom and grace.

Engaging in Creative Expression: Creativity is a powerful way to contribute to the sacred symphony. Whether through art, music, writing, or other forms of creative expression, we can explore and communicate the harmony of the universe in ways that resonate with others. Creative expression allows us to tap into the deeper currents of the quantum field and bring forth new ideas, visions, and possibilities. By engaging in creative activities, we add our unique voice to the sacred symphony, contributing to the collective evolution of consciousness.

Practicing Compassionate Action: Compassionate action is another essential component of the sacred symphony. By acting with kindness, empathy, and love, we contribute to the creation of a more harmonious and compassionate world. This involves being mindful of the impact of our actions on others and making choices that support the well-being of all beings. Compassionate action is not just about doing good deeds; it is about living in a way that reflects our awareness of the interconnectedness of all life.

Fostering Community and Connection: The sacred symphony is not a solo performance; it is a collective endeavour. By fostering community and connection, we create spaces where individuals can come together to explore, practice, and live the principles of quantum spirituality. These communities provide support, inspiration, and collaboration, helping to amplify the harmony of the sacred symphony. Whether through formal groups or informal gatherings, fostering connection helps to build a culture of harmony and unity, where the sacred symphony can flourish.

Aligning with the Flow of the Universe: Finally, contributing to the sacred symphony involves aligning with the flow of the universe. This means trusting in the deeper order that guides the unfolding of reality and being open to the changes and transformations that life brings. By surrendering to the flow of life, we allow ourselves to be guided by the harmony of the universe, contributing to the sacred symphony with ease and grace. This practice helps us to let go of resistance and to embrace the natural rhythms of life, living in alignment with the deeper truths of existence.

The Future of the Sacred Symphony: A Vision of Unity and Harmony

The sacred symphony we contribute to today will shape the world of tomorrow. By living in alignment with quantum principles and spiritual values, we can create a future that is more harmonious, compassionate, and enlightened. This future is one where science and spirituality are not seen as separate domains but are integrated into a holistic understanding of the universe.

A World of Unity and Cooperation: In the future envisioned by the sacred symphony, unity and cooperation will be the guiding principles of human society. The recognition of our interconnectedness will lead to policies and practices that prioritize the well-being of all beings, fostering a culture of care and respect. This will be a world where differences are celebrated, where diversity is seen as a strength, and where collaboration and cooperation are the norm. By embracing unity and cooperation, future generations will create a society that reflects the harmony and beauty of the cosmos.

The Evolution of Consciousness: The sacred symphony also envisions the continued evolution of human consciousness. As more people awaken to the deeper truths of quantum spirituality, there will be a collective shift towards higher states of awareness and understanding. This evolution of consciousness will lead to new ways of thinking, being, and relating, transforming not only individual lives but also the structures and systems that govern society. The continued evolution of consciousness will be a key driver of the sacred symphony, ensuring that future generations are equipped to navigate the complexities of the quantum world.

A Legacy of Harmony and Beauty: Ultimately, the sacred symphony is a legacy of harmony and beauty, a testament to the power of integrating science and spirituality. It is a reminder that we are not separate from the universe but are integral parts of the cosmic dance. By living in alignment with the sacred symphony, we create a legacy that reflects the unity, beauty, and order of the cosmos, guiding humanity towards a future of harmony and enlightenment.

Embracing the Sacred Symphony: A Call to Harmony

As we conclude this final chapter, we are called to embrace the sacred symphony, to live in alignment with the harmony of the universe, and to contribute to the integration of science and spirituality in the world. This is not just a personal journey; it is a collective endeavour, a call to action

that invites us to come together as a global community, united by our shared commitment to the principles of quantum spirituality.

The sacred symphony is a journey of discovery, awakening, and transformation. It challenges us to live with greater awareness, intention, and alignment with the deeper rhythms of the universe. As we continue this journey, let us remember that we are not alone; we are part of a vast, interconnected web of life, a cosmic dance that has been unfolding for eons and will continue to unfold long after we are gone.

Let us embrace the sacred symphony with joy and gratitude, knowing that by doing so, we are contributing to a future that is filled with harmony, beauty, and light. And let us pass this torch to future generations, ensuring that the harmony of the sacred symphony continues to inspire, guide, and uplift all who come after us.

The sacred symphony represents the harmonious integration of science and spirituality, a vision of the universe where the material and the mystical are seen as complementary aspects of the same cosmic dance. By living in alignment with quantum principles and spiritual values, we can contribute to this symphony, creating a world that reflects the unity, beauty, and order of the cosmos. As we explore the deeper dimensions of quantum spirituality, we are invited to embrace the sacred symphony as a call to harmony, a call to live in a way that honours the interconnectedness of all life and contributes to the collective evolution of humanity.

CHAPTER 29: THE QUANTUM HOMECOMING: RETURNING TO THE SOURCE

In the silent depths of the cosmos, where the mysteries of existence converge, there is a place—a place not of physical dimensions but of profound significance, where all journeys begin and where all paths ultimately lead. This place is the source, the origin of all that is, a wellspring of energy, consciousness, and creation. Inspired by Michael Talbot's Mysticism and the New Physics, this chapter delves into the concept of returning to the source, a journey that is both scientific and spiritual. It explores how understanding our origins through the lens of quantum spirituality can lead to a profound sense of homecoming, peace, and unity with the cosmos.

The Source: The Origin of All Existence

In the vast tapestry of the universe, everything emerges from a single point of origin—a source that gives rise to all forms, energies, and consciousness. This source is often described in mystical traditions as the Divine, the Absolute, or the Ground of Being. In the realm of quantum physics, this source can be understood as the quantum field, a primordial sea of potentialities from which all particles, forces, and realities emerge.

The source is not just a starting point in time or space; it is an ever-present reality, the underlying foundation of all existence. It is the place where the visible and the invisible, the material and the spiritual, the known and the unknown converge. The source is the origin of all creation, the point of unity from which the diversity of the universe unfolds.

In quantum spirituality, the journey to return to the source is a journey of remembering—remembering who we are, where we come from, and what connects us to all that is. This journey is not about traveling to a distant place; it is about turning inward, recognizing that the source is not something external but something that resides within us, as the essence of our being.

The Scientific and Spiritual Path to the Source

The journey to the source can be approached from both a scientific and a spiritual perspective, each offering unique insights and pathways to understanding our origins and our ultimate destination.

The Scientific Path: Understanding the Quantum Field: In quantum physics, the quantum field represents the source of all physical reality. It is the foundation of everything that exists, the field of infinite possibilities where all potential states of matter and energy reside before manifesting in the physical world. Understanding the quantum field is akin to tracing the roots of existence, uncovering the principles that govern the birth of particles, the formation of atoms, and the evolution of the cosmos.

The quantum field is not just a theoretical construct; it is a living, dynamic reality that connects all things in the universe. By studying the quantum field, scientists have uncovered the profound interconnectedness of all particles and forces, revealing that everything in the universe is related, entangled in a web of relationships that transcend space and time. This understanding brings us closer to the source, illuminating the deep unity that underlies the diversity of the material world.

The Spiritual Path: The Mystical Journey to Unity: Mystical traditions across cultures and religions speak of a journey to the source, a return to the Divine, where the soul reunites with its origin. This journey is described as a path of enlightenment, awakening, or liberation, where the individual transcends the limitations of the ego and merges with the universal consciousness. The spiritual path to the source involves practices such as meditation, contemplation, prayer, and surrender, which help the seeker to dissolve the illusion of separateness and experience the oneness of all existence.

The mystical journey is not about escaping the world

but about transcending the illusion of duality and recognizing the unity that pervades all things. It is a journey of deep inner transformation, where the seeker discovers that the source is not something distant or unattainable but is the very essence of their being. By returning to the source, the mystic experiences a profound sense of homecoming, where all longing and searching come to an end, and the soul rests in the peace of its true nature.

The Quantum Homecoming: Finding Peace in Unity

The concept of a quantum homecoming combines the scientific understanding of the quantum field with the spiritual experience of returning to the source. It is the recognition that our true home is not a physical place, but a state of being, a deep connection to the underlying reality that sustains and unites all of existence.

The Peace of Unity: One of the most profound aspects of the quantum homecoming is the experience of peace that comes from recognizing our unity with the source. In this state of unity, the boundaries that separate us from others and from the world dissolve, and we experience a deep sense of belonging and connection. This peace is not just a temporary feeling of contentment; it is a lasting sense of wholeness that arises from knowing that we are part of a greater whole, that we are connected to the source of all life.

The End of Seeking: The quantum homecoming also brings an end to the restless seeking that characterizes much of human life. When we recognize that we are already connected to the source, that we are already at home in the universe, the need to search for meaning, purpose, or fulfilment outside of ourselves falls away. This realization allows us to live with greater ease and simplicity, trusting that everything we need is already within us, and that the universe is always guiding us towards our highest good.

The Joy of Presence: Finally, the quantum homecoming brings us into a state of joyful presence, where we can fully experience the beauty and wonder of life. When we are connected to the source, we are no longer distracted by fears or anxieties about the future or regrets about the past. Instead, we are able to live fully in the present moment, appreciating the gift of life and the miracle of existence. This joyful presence is not a fleeting emotion but a deep, abiding state of being that reflects our connection to the source.

Living the Quantum Homecoming: Practical Steps for Daily Life

The experience of a quantum homecoming is not reserved for mystical experiences or scientific discoveries; it is something that can be cultivated in daily life. By living in alignment with the principles of quantum spirituality, we can experience the peace, unity, and joy that come from returning to the source.

Mindful Awareness of Interconnectedness: One of the most important practices for living the quantum homecoming is cultivating mindful awareness of our interconnectedness with all life. This involves recognizing that every thought, word, and action has an impact on the world around us, and that we are part of a vast, interconnected web of relationships. By practicing mindfulness, we can tune into the deeper rhythms of the universe and live in a way that reflects our unity with the source.

Embracing Stillness and Silence: Another key practice is embracing stillness and silence. In the stillness of meditation or contemplation, we can connect with the source within us, experiencing the peace and presence that come from being in harmony with the universe. By creating moments of stillness in our daily lives, we can cultivate a deeper connection to the source and experience the joy of simply being.

Living with Gratitude and Reverence: Gratitude and reverence are essential qualities for living the quantum homecoming. By cultivating a sense of gratitude for the gift of life and a reverence for the mystery of existence, we can live in a way that honours our connection to the source. This practice helps us to appreciate the beauty and wonder of the world around us and to live with a sense of awe and humility.

Serving Others as an Expression of Unity: Finally, serving others is a powerful way to live the quantum homecoming. When we recognize that we are all connected, that we all share the same source, we naturally feel called to help and support others. By serving others with love and compassion, we express our unity with the source and contribute to the creation of a more harmonious and peaceful world.

The Journey of the Quantum Homecoming: Embracing Our True Nature

As we conclude this chapter, we are invited to embrace the journey of the quantum homecoming, to return to the source both scientifically and spiritually, and to live in a way that reflects our true nature. This journey is not about reaching a destination; it is about awakening to the reality that we are already home, that we are already connected to the source of all life.

The journey of the quantum homecoming is a path of self-discovery, where we explore the depths of our being and reconnect with the essence of who we are. It is a journey that challenges us to let go of the illusions of separateness and to embrace the unity that underlies all existence. As we continue this journey, let us remember that we are not alone; we are part of a vast, interconnected web of life, a cosmic dance that has been unfolding for eons and will continue to unfold long after we are gone.

Let us embrace the quantum homecoming with joy and gratitude, knowing that by doing so, we are returning to our true nature, experiencing the peace, unity, and joy that come from being in harmony with the source. And let us share this homecoming with others, inviting them to join us on the journey of quantum spirituality, where we can all find our way back to the source.

The quantum homecoming represents the journey of returning to the source, both scientifically and spiritually. By understanding our origins through the lens of quantum spirituality, we can experience a profound sense of homecoming, peace, and unity with the cosmos. As we explore the deeper dimensions of quantum spirituality, we are invited to embrace the quantum homecoming as a path to discovering our true nature and living in harmony with the source of all existence.

CHAPTER 30: THE SACRED QUANTUM REVELATION: A FINAL REFLECTION

In the closing notes of our journey, where the echoes of science and spirituality converge into a unified symphony, there lies a revelation—a sacred quantum revelation that encompasses all we have explored, all we have pondered, and all we have become. Inspired by Michael Talbot's The Holographic Universe, this final chapter offers a deep, poetic reflection on the journey of quantum spirituality. It revisits the central themes of the book, weaving together the threads of the scientific and the sacred into a tapestry of profound understanding, offering a conclusion that is not an end, but a new beginning.

The Holographic Universe: A Reflection of the Whole

As we reflect upon the journey we have taken, we

return to the concept of the holographic universe—a universe in which every part contains the whole, where each fragment of reality reflects the totality. This idea, so beautifully encapsulated in Talbot's work, serves as a fitting metaphor for the integration of science and spirituality. Just as a hologram contains the entire image within every smaller piece, so too does the universe contain the divine within every aspect of creation.

This understanding invites us to see the world not as a collection of separate, isolated parts, but as a unified whole, where every particle, every thought, every being is an expression of the infinite. The holographic nature of the universe reflects the deep truth that the sacred is not something distant or separate, but is present in every moment, every experience, and every aspect of our lives. It is a reminder that we are not merely observers of the universe, but integral parts of the cosmic dance, where the scientific and the sacred are intertwined in a seamless, harmonious whole.

The Journey of Quantum Spirituality: Revisiting the Central Themes

As we reach the conclusion of our exploration, it is fitting to revisit the central themes of quantum spirituality, reflecting on how they have guided us through this journey of discovery and awakening.

The Dance of the Quantum and the Sacred: We began our journey by exploring the dance between the quantum world and the sacred, discovering how modern physics and ancient spiritual wisdom converge to reveal a deeper reality. This dance is a dynamic interplay, where the material and the mystical, the seen and the unseen, come together in a harmonious embrace. It is a reminder that the boundaries we perceive between science and spirituality are illusions, and that the true nature of reality is one of unity and interconnectedness.

The Unseen Web of Reality: We delved into the idea of an interconnected universe, where all life and consciousness are woven together in a cosmic web. This unseen web, the Divine Matrix, is the foundation of our existence, connecting us to one another and to the greater whole. It is through this web that we experience the resonance of love, compassion, and unity, recognizing that our actions, thoughts, and intentions have far-reaching effects, shaping not only our lives but the fabric of reality itself.

The Holographic Nature of the Universe: We explored the concept of the holographic universe, where every part contains the whole, and where the boundaries between self and other, mind and matter, dissolve. This understanding challenges us to see ourselves as reflections of the divine, to recognize that the universe is not outside of us, but within us, and that we are co-creators of our reality, shaping the world through our consciousness.

The Quantum Mind and the Ground of Being: We journeyed into the depths of consciousness, discovering that mind, rather than matter, is the primary substance of the universe. This realization invites us to awaken to our true nature, to recognize that we are not merely physical beings, but spiritual beings connected to the source of all existence. It is through this awakening that we experience the peace and unity that come from aligning with the ground of being, the source from which all life flows.

The Quantum Leap from Mind to Matter: We explored the relationship between mind and matter, discovering how our thoughts and intentions shape the physical world. This quantum leap, from mind to matter, is a powerful reminder of our creative potential, inviting us to use our consciousness to manifest a reality that reflects the divine. It is a call to live with intention, to align our actions with our highest values, and to contribute to the creation of a more harmonious and compassionate world.

The Sacred Science: We ventured into the sacred science of the quantum field, exploring concepts such as the Akashic Field, quantum consciousness, and the field of infinite possibilities. These explorations revealed the deep connections between science and spirituality, showing us that the universe is a living, dynamic reality, where consciousness and energy interact in profound ways. This sacred science is not just a way of understanding the world; it is a path to experiencing the divine, to living in harmony with the deeper rhythms of the universe.

The Path to Enlightenment: We embarked on the path to enlightenment, using quantum consciousness as a guide to explore the inner realms of the self. This journey of self-discovery, transformation, and awakening led us to the recognition that enlightenment is not a distant goal, but a process of realizing our true nature and living in alignment with the truth of our interconnectedness. It is a path that challenges us to transcend the limitations of the ego, to embrace the unity of all life, and to experience the peace and joy that come from living in harmony with the universe.

The Integration of Science and Spirit: We explored the alchemy of integrating science and spirituality, discovering how this integration leads to profound transformations in our understanding of the universe and our place within it. This integration is the essence of quantum spirituality, a holistic approach to life that honours both the material and the mystical, the scientific and the sacred. It is through this integration that we can create a life that reflects the beauty, harmony, and unity of the cosmos.

Living the Quantum Spirituality: We turned our attention to practical ways of living the principles of quantum spirituality, exploring rituals, mindfulness, relationships, compassion, and creation. These practices are not just ways of improving our lives; they are paths to aligning with the quantum field, to living in harmony with the divine, and to contributing to the creation of a more enlightened and harmonious world.

The Sacred Future and Legacy: Finally, we envisioned a sacred future, where humanity evolves through the integration of quantum science and spirituality, creating a world of unity, cooperation, and compassion. We explored the idea of a quantum legacy, recognizing our responsibility to pass on the knowledge of quantum spirituality to future generations, ensuring that the light of this wisdom continues to guide humanity towards a more enlightened and harmonious future.

The Final Revelation: Unity in Diversity

As we bring our journey to a close, we arrive at a final

revelation—a revelation that ties together all we have explored, all we have learned, and all we have become. This revelation is the recognition of unity in diversity, the understanding that the diversity of the universe is not a sign of separation, but a reflection of the infinite possibilities contained within the unity of the whole.

The holographic nature of the universe teaches us that every part contains the whole, that every being, every particle, every thought is a reflection of the greater reality. This understanding invites us to see the world in a new light, to recognize that the differences we perceive are not obstacles to unity, but expressions of the infinite creativity of the cosmos.

In this final reflection, we are called to embrace the diversity of the world, to honour the uniqueness of each being, each culture, each tradition, while recognizing the underlying unity that connects us all. This unity in diversity is the essence of the sacred quantum revelation, a truth that transcends the boundaries of science and spirituality, leading us to a deeper understanding of the universe and our place within it.

A New Beginning: The Journey Continues

As we conclude this chapter, we recognize that this is not the end of our journey, but the beginning of a new one. The journey of quantum spirituality is a journey without end, a continuous process of discovery, awakening, and transformation. Each step we take brings us closer to the source, deeper into the mystery of existence, and more aligned with the harmony of the cosmos.

This journey invites us to live with greater awareness,

intention, and love, to contribute to the sacred symphony of the universe, and to pass on the torch of quantum spirituality to future generations. It is a journey that challenges us to see the world through the eyes of unity, to embrace the sacredness of all life, and to live in harmony with the deeper rhythms of existence.

As we step into this new beginning, let us carry with us the insights, the wisdom, and the revelations we have gained on this journey. Let us continue to explore, to question, and to grow, knowing that we are part of a vast, interconnected web of life, a cosmic dance that has been unfolding for eons and will continue to unfold long after we are gone.

Let us embrace the sacred quantum revelation with joy and gratitude, knowing that by doing so, we are contributing to a future that is filled with harmony, beauty, and light. And let us walk this path together, as co-creators of a reality that reflects the divine order of the universe, a reality where science and spirituality are united in a sacred symphony of existence.

The sacred quantum revelation is a profound understanding of the unity that underlies the diversity of the universe. By integrating science and spirituality, we can create a life that reflects the beauty, harmony, and unity of the cosmos. As we conclude this journey of quantum spirituality, we are invited to embrace this final revelation as a new beginning, a call to live in harmony with the deeper rhythms of the universe and to contribute to the creation of a more enlightened and harmonious world.

EPILOGUE: THE ENDLESS DANCE OF QUANTUM AND SPIRIT

In the infinite theatre of the cosmos, where galaxies spin like graceful dancers across the velvet curtain of space, a dance unfolds—a dance as ancient as time, as mysterious as the breath of life itself. It is the endless dance of quantum and spirit, a dance that transcends the boundaries of the material and the mystical, weaving them together in a symphony of existence that is both seen and unseen, known and unknowable.

This dance is not merely a cosmic spectacle; it is the very essence of reality, the rhythm that pulses through every atom, every star, every living being. It is the heartbeat of the universe, a continuous ebb and flow of creation and dissolution, of order and chaos, of light and shadow. In this dance, the quantum world and the spiritual realm intertwine, each reflecting the other in a mirror of infinite depth.

The dance of quantum and spirit is a journey—a journey that beckons us to step beyond the confines of our limited understanding and into the boundless possibilities of the unknown. It is a journey that invites us to explore not only the vastness of the cosmos but also the depths of our own consciousness, to discover the hidden connections that bind us to the universe and to each other.

As we reach the culmination of this exploration, we stand on the threshold of a profound revelation: the realization that the dance of quantum and spirit is not something that happens outside of us, but something that unfolds within us, through us, and as us. We are not merely spectators in this grand cosmic ballet; we are participants, co-creators in the ever-evolving story of existence.

This dance is the dance of life itself, the dance of being and becoming, of unity and diversity, of the finite and the infinite. It is a dance that takes place in every moment, in every breath, in every thought and feeling. It is the dance of the stars and the galaxies, of the waves and the particles, of the mind and the heart. It is the dance of love, of joy, of sorrow, of wonder.

In the quiet moments of reflection, when the noise of the world fades away and we are left alone with our thoughts, we can feel the gentle rhythm of this dance. It is the rhythm of the quantum field, the invisible web that connects all things, the pulse of the universe that beats in time with our own hearts. It is a rhythm that reminds us that we are not separate from the world, but part of it, woven into the fabric of reality by threads of light and energy, of consciousness and spirit.

The endless dance of quantum and spirit is a dance of paradoxes, where the smallest particle contains the entire universe, where the past, present, and future are all one, where the observer and the observed are inseparable. It is a dance that challenges us to embrace the mystery of existence, to live in the space between certainty and uncertainty, between knowing and unknowing, between the tangible and the transcendent.

As we reflect on the journey we have taken, we are reminded that this dance is not something that can be fully understood or explained, but something that must be experienced, felt, lived. It is a dance that calls us to be present, to be open, to be curious, to be courageous. It is a dance that invites us to explore the depths of our own being, to discover the divine within ourselves and within all things.

This dance is the dance of the universe, a dance that has been unfolding for billions of years and will continue to unfold long after we are gone. It is a dance that connects us to the stars, to the earth, to each other. It is a dance that reminds us that we are all part of the same cosmic story, that our lives are intertwined with the fabric of the universe, that we are all dancers in the great ballet of existence.

And as we continue on our own journeys, let us carry with us the spirit of this dance, the spirit of wonder and exploration, of openness and humility, of love and compassion. Let us remember that the dance of quantum and spirit is not a destination, but a path, a way of being in the world that honours the mystery and beauty of life.

In every moment, in every choice, in every interaction, we are given the opportunity to dance—to move in harmony with the rhythms of the universe, to create beauty and meaning, to connect with others in deep and profound ways. This dance is a gift, a sacred gift that we are called to embrace, to cherish, to share.

As we step back into the world, let us do so with a renewed sense of purpose and inspiration. Let us continue to explore the mysteries of the universe, to seek out the connections between the quantum and the spiritual, to live in a way that honours the sacredness of all life. Let us be guided by the rhythm of the dance, by the wisdom of the universe, by the light that shines within and around us.

For in this endless dance of quantum and spirit, we find not only the answers to our deepest questions, but also the joy of being, the peace of unity, and the wonder of the infinite. We find the sacred in the ordinary, the extraordinary in the everyday, the divine in the dance of life itself.

And so, the dance continues, an eternal movement of quantum and spirit, guiding us through the mysteries of life and the cosmos. It is a dance that never ends, a dance that we are all a part of a dance that invites us to live fully, to love deeply, to be present in every moment.

May we always be open to the dance, always be willing to step into the unknown, always be ready to embrace the beauty and the mystery of existence. And may we carry the spirit of this dance with us, wherever we go, in all that we do, in all that we are.

For the dance of quantum and spirit is the dance of life, the dance of the universe, the dance of the divine. And in this dance, we find our true home, our true purpose, our true selves.

The endless dance of quantum and spirit is a poetic reflection on the ongoing interplay between science and spirituality, a dance that invites us to explore the mysteries of the universe and our own consciousness. As you continue your journey of discovery, may you be inspired by the beauty and wonder of this dance, and may you find joy, peace, and meaning in the sacred rhythms of life.

ACKNOWLEDGEMENTS

'The Journey of Quantum Spirituality: A Journey Beyond The Visible' has been a profound journey, one that would not have been possible without the support, wisdom, and encouragement of many extraordinary individuals.

First and foremost, I would like to express my deepest gratitude to my family. Your unwavering support and love have been the foundation upon which this book was built. To my parents, who instilled in me a deep curiosity for the mysteries of the universe, and to my children, whose wonder and imagination continue to inspire me daily—I am forever grateful.

I extend my heartfelt thanks to my mentors and colleagues in both the scientific and spiritual communities. Your insights and guidance have been invaluable in shaping the ideas presented in this book. Special thanks to my editor, whose keen eye and thoughtful feedback helped refine and enhance the narrative, and to my publisher, Irene Minds, for believing in this project and bringing it to life.

To the many authors, scientists, and spiritual leaders whose work has influenced and inspired this book, I owe a great debt. Your groundbreaking research and timeless wisdom provided the foundation upon which this exploration of quantum spirituality was built.

Finally, to my readers—thank you for embarking on this journey with me. It is my hope that the ideas presented here will inspire you to explore the profound connections between science and spirituality and to continue your own journey beyond the visible.

COPYRIGHT INFORMATION

The Journey of Quantum Spirituality
© 2024 by Dr. Bhaskar Bora
All rights reserved.

No part of this book may be reproduced, distributed, or transmitted in any form or by any means, including photocopying, recording, or other electronic or mechanical methods, without the prior written permission of the publisher, except in the case of brief quotations embodied in critical reviews and certain other non-commercial uses permitted by copyright law.

For permission requests, write to the publisher at the address below:

Irene Minds

Published by Irene Minds, 2024

DISCLAIMER

This book is intended for educational and informational purposes only. The content within Quantum Spirituality: A Journey Beyond The Visible represents the author's exploration of the intersection between quantum science and spirituality. It is not intended as a definitive guide to quantum mechanics, nor as a substitute for professional scientific, medical, or spiritual advice.

The concepts and interpretations presented in this book are based on the author's research, insights, and personal experiences. Readers are encouraged to explore these ideas with an open mind and to engage in their own critical thinking and exploration. The author and publisher assume no responsibility for any errors or omissions, or for any actions taken based on the information contained in this book.

All references to existing works, authors, and scientific principles are cited in good faith, with full respect for the original creators. The author has endeavoured to credit all sources accurately. If any copyright concerns arise, please contact the publisher for resolution.

Printed in Dunstable, United Kingdom